Behold a Tree

**Roots of Resilience
Branches of Hope**

by Jewell Utt

Behold a Tree:
Roots of Resilience Branches of Hope
by Jewell Utt

Copyright © 2024
All rights reserved.

Library of Congress Number: 2024940568
International Standard Book Number: 978-1-60126-938-6

Published by
Masthof Press

219 Mill Road | Morgantown, PA 19543-9516
www.Masthof.com

Table of Contents

Endorsements vii
Dedication xi
Foreword xiii
Preface xiv

Chapter 1: The Angel Tree
   A Legacy to Behold 2
   The Angel Oak 5
   The Trees Shake Before the Wind 6

Chapter 2: Anne Frank
   The Secret Annex 12
   The Chestnut Tree 15
   The Early Church 17

Chapter 3: Sir Isaac Newton
   A Great Thinker 24
   The Flower of Kent Apple Tree 26
   Sin 27

Chapter 4: Joyce Kilmer
   I Think That I May Never See 34
   Poplar Cove 37
   Only God 38
   Trees 38

Chapter 5: Thomas Hardy
A Tender Embrace 42
The Ash Tree 45
Character 46

Chapter 6: Betsy Ross
Fact or Lore? 52
The Great White Oak—Gone But Not Forgotten ... 54
What Is Truth? 55

Chapter 7: The Devil Tree
The Evil Twin 60
Trees Versus Stars 62
Trees in the Bible 63

Chapter 8: The Belvidere Shoe Tree
Belvidere Shoe Tree 70
A Sappy Solution 72
New Shoes Please 73

Chapter 9: Paul Smith College
The Leaning Pine 80
The White Pine 82
Justice for the Pine 83

Chapter 10: Methuselah
Methuselah—The Man 90
The Bristlecone Pine 91
The Price of Fame 92

Chapter 11: The Hawaiian Kukui—Polynesia
Henry Obookiah 98
The Kukui Tree 100
The Yoke of Oppression 101

Chapter 12: The Tree of Life
Etz Chaim 108
The Balboa Tree 110
Tree of Life Stories 112

Chapter 13: The Specialty of Three
The Three Trees 122
The Christmas Tree 123
On the Count of Tree 125

Chapter 14: The Final Three
The Crooked Tree 132
No Trees! 133
List of State Trees 134

Endnotes 139
Branches of Thanksgiving 143
Community Blend Incorporated 144
About the Author 145

Endorsements

The author has progressed from *Consider the Birds* into their habitat, trees. In her newest book, *Behold a Tree*, we see yet more pictures of the life lessons God provides for everyone who is searching. Trees are a reminder of resilience as they stand strong through the storms of life, providing respite and shade during the heat of the day and encouragement during difficult times.

Jewell has condensed her extensive research into a book for us to enjoy the beauty, strength, and endurance of another one of God's creations and points us to His comforting and transformative love. Enjoy your read!

- VAL SARKADY
Friend, Proof Reader, Behold Prayer Team

In her last book, Jewell combined bird watching and God in a unique way. She does the same with her newest book on trees. Trees are an essential part of our environment and I'm glad to see personal stories and trees highlighted in this way. Chapter nine features my personal tree story; the sad story of the leaning pine from Paul Smith College.

- RON COLLINS
Forestry, Wood Science Engineering, Syracuse University, NY
College of Forestry, Paul Smith College

A masterful blend of theology, history, literature, and nature. This book is captivating. It invites the reader to draw connections they might not otherwise see and inspires us to do the same with the multiple facets of our lives and our faith. Jewell has authored a thought-provoking book that will leave you marveling about God, His creation (including us), and the intricate ways He weaves the two.

- TONI SAMUELS
Hawk Pointe Writers Group
North America Communications Manager for Global Engineering

This book is for everyone who seeks beauty and refreshment. God gave us the gift of trees to clean our air, give us shade and feed the animals. Jewell weaves a tapestry of God's goodness through scripture, human interest stories, and information about trees. These magnificent products of creation provide encouragement during our hardest times. In the end God's gift of Jesus Christ is His greatest gift to all. This book inspires us to connect with nature and our Creator.

- KATHY HALPIN
*Washington Borough Shade Tree Commission,
Board President Warren County Habitat for Humanity*

Trees surrounded me, in one form or another, for most of my life. My first experience was when my father, uncle and grandfather made showroom furniture for businesses in NYC. As a career, I taught high school woodshop, teaching students about the properties of different woods. After I married, my father-in-law had numerous fruit trees, which I learned how to maintain, harvest, and preserve the fruit. God has provided us with the tremendous gift of trees. They give us the purified air we breathe, food to eat, shelter/warmth and even careers. This book shows us the importance of God's creation and how it has affected us since the beginning of time.

- RALPH FIORE
*Industrial Education Teacher,
New Jersey Forestry Association Member*

Walking through the woods is a time for connections. Connections with family and friends without the distraction of technology. Connections with the past as we admire majestic old trees and all they have endured over many decades. Connections with God, as we enjoy His beautiful and peaceful creation and reflect upon our purpose in life.

Behold a Tree expands on those connections by sharing stories and Bible verses about how trees have inspired others. For the times when we cannot get out for a walk in the woods, this book can help us step out of our busy digital worlds and reflect upon those natural connections that God intended.

- Daryl Detrick
Educator, Environmental Club founder,
Washington Township Trail Maintenance 20+yrs

Once again, Jewell has assembled historical accounts, interesting facts, and the inspiration of nature to engage our hearts and highlight the creativity of God. As trees provide food, shelter, protection, and beauty, these stories show how God works as our shelter in the storm, our protection from the heated blasts of life and the beauty that uplifts us in a world of disappointments.

- Deborah Gatz
Hawk Pointe Writers Group,
Community Blend Prayer Team, Friend

God often uses the wonder of His creation to speak truth into our hearts. How fitting that Jewell has beautifully called our attention to the magnificence of trees. With great care and insight, she challenges us to ponder how trees point us to the Lord and illustrate His Word. Each chapter provides deeply personal scripture and fully relatable stories due to the artful way she has woven her touching narratives around trees. I look forward to heart changes and a deeper understanding of God, which can be experienced with the encouragement provided by this amazing book.

- Diane O'Brien
Teacher, Student, Contributor,
Community Blend Prayer Team

DEDICATION

This book is lovingly dedicated to my family tree. The daily prayer support of my siblings, gleaned from our rich Christian heritage, is a legacy passed on to future generations. We are abundantly blessed. Craig, my personal oak, and saplings Brandon, Jordan, and Jonathan have inspired my life through their diligence and servant hearts.

My grandmother played a significant role in my life. She cared for me as a newborn while mom paved our family's way to the United States. Once we were all reunited, Gama and I shared a room until I was ten. She poured faith and strength into my life, a legacy I hope to pass on to my granddaughter, Aria Joy.

Foreword

Having enjoyed the natural beauty of her home area in northwest New Jersey for decades, Jewell captures the magic of God's creation and His creatures in her writing. A logical sequel to *Consider the Birds, Behold a Tree* celebrates the variety and uniqueness of many trees native to her environment. People native to the area will enjoy a real sense of local color, as they learn about the wonder of these unique specimens they might have encountered repeatedly without appreciating the history. Not only native trees, but trees from all over the United States and the world relate stories of God's provision to all people.

From these stories of a variety of majestic trees, some older than a millennium, Jewell presents eye-opening lessons about ourselves. These magnificent denizens of the world around us demonstrate strength, perseverance, focus and beauty—virtues they willingly share—if we but open our eyes. Nothing should lift our hearts to worship more than God's creation. Yet Romans 1 tells us many choose to worship the creation rather than the Creator who is greatly to be praised.

God's handiwork certainly can steal our breath and bring us to our knees in wonder. Surely, its purpose is to display His glory—the sum of His characteristics—and His creative fingerprints. Our appropriate response should be worship, praise and thanksgiving. This little gem is full of reflections that can cause us to do just that. Let us allow the majesty of creation to draw us closer to our Creator, who is ever to be praised.

- MAUREEN BRACKSHAW
Teacher of Composition and Rhetoric
Jewell's sister, editor, and friend

Preface

The trees are still today. Normally, they are waving in the wind. I wave back and if no one is looking I imitate their motion with my whole body. It refreshes my spirit. The crackle under foot, fresh fragrance of leaves, and rhythmic sway all mesmerize me. My every sense stimulated and alive. I am at peace surrounded by trees, which is good, since I live surrounded by trees.

Growing up I had a special tree in a secret place where I would escape to write and hang out with friends. I nested there, bordering my space with rocks, building a center fire pit, and of course carving my name in the tree. I chose that special tree for my chair. The roots came up so high it created a seat complete with armrests just for me.

In my room, I drew a wall-sized tree with branches extended up and out. Anyone who visited got to write a few words or just sign their name. Seedlings from my childhood home are planted all around our property, lovingly transferred by my parents. Three maples were planted in honor of my three sons. All were different types of maple seedlings. One was constantly eaten by the deer and would not grow. So, we replaced it with an evergreen sapling received from their fourth-grade teacher.

Trees are good for the environment exchanging carbon dioxide for oxygen and cleaning pollution from the air. Their majestic canopy creates a natural filter for the sun and rain. But … they also produce pollen. Even though pollen causes allergies, as it is carried by the wind or insects, it provides needed nourishment for trees.

Like humans, trees face adversities of all types. The

weather is not always kind. Trees must withstand brutal storms, frigid temperatures, and scorching climates; yet the strongest trees have withstood the harshest climates. Ironically, they are strengthened by adversity in the same way humans are shaped by challenges. Yet, they continue to grow and clean our air, bearing fruit in season and out.

Also, like humans, not all trees are healthy and capable of contributing positively to their environment. Some are infested with insects or diseases that eventually kill them. And not all substances released by trees are healthy. Though trees purify our air, they also release unwholesome particles like volatiles. Volatiles are a group of chemical elements that vaporize into the air.

Trees release volatiles to ward off insect attacks. It is a defense mechanism they use for themselves and their forests. Like an SOS chain, they send out signals to other trees, which then send their own signals. Volatiles also act as a call for help to wasps, ladybugs and larger insects who gladly cooperate by eating their attackers.

Clearly, trees work in community to keep each other safe and healthy. They take our bad air and give us oxygen. We breathe out carbon dioxide, which they need. This is a symbiotic relationship created by God, and a pattern demonstrated by Jesus. He took our sin and gave us His righteousness in exchange. May we live lives of gratitude and thanksgiving to the Creator, who gave us a miraculous creation to tend and enjoy.

Love and Blessings,
Jewell Utt
Communityblend.org
Jewellutt.com

Reflection questions
are found at the end of each
chapter as well as a
coloring page to let your
creative juices flow.

Chapter 1

The Angel Tree

A Legacy to Behold

*She is a tree of life to those who lay hold of her;
those who hold her fast are called blessed.*
PROVERBS 3:18

Imagine if your smallest, seemingly insignificant decision, could spring forth a legacy of hope a millennium later. The Angel Tree set in Bay St. Louis, Mississippi, tells such a story. Its legacy stands as a symbol of hope and a reminder that our smallest decisions can yield the greatest results.

Ovenia de Montluzin lived in a palatial home, built in the 1890s, regally set on the Mississippi coast. The house showcased high ceilings, crystal chandeliers, an array of antiques, and eight bedrooms with private baths. Financially blessed, her family donated money to the town to preserve a portion of the land. As a result, Demontluzin Avenue was named in their honor.

As crews were clearing the way, Ovenia spotted an oak sapling they intended to remove. Knowing the oak would grow into a mighty tree, she wanted to see it from her kitchen window over years to come. She ran out and implored them not to disturb it and after a successful appeal, they agreed to leave it standing. From that decision sprouted a tree of life.

On August 29, 2005, Hurricane Katrina hit the Bay St. Louis area in Mississippi. Most people were aware and concerned about New Orleans, but Hurricane Katrina also devastated Mississippi. A 35–40-foot storm surge plowed into the coastline at the mouth of the Pearl River, resulting in the death of 238 people and billions of dollars in property damage. Every county in Mississippi was declared a disaster zone. Rebuilding the coast took years and parts of the state have yet to recover.

The de Montluzin home had been transformed into a bed and breakfast sheltering people from storms in the past. So, when news of Katrina hit, four people decided to stay the course and take their chances there. As the storm grew worse, water began to rise in the house, and they realized they had to evacuate . . . when one of them spotted the tree. The very oak tree that Ovenia fought to keep rooted, now so many years later, stood as a beacon of hope and survival for the stranded group.

Amid ferocious winds and crashing water, two men and two women struggled to latch on to the tree. Battered by the storm, one of the women was taken away by currents; but later found refuge at a neighboring home.

Of the three that fought their way up the tree, one woman had a small dog tucked in her shirt. She is the current owner of the bed and breakfast, and as a survivor lives to tell the tale. The group clung tightly to the tree for hours, and during that time the little dog, sensing imminent danger, stayed completely still. When large waves were approaching, someone would warn the others to hang tight.

During grueling hours, holding on for dear life, the group witnessed the destruction of the town around them. One of their darkest moments was witnessing the inn lifted off its foundation and swept away by the force of the water. Finally, when the eye of the storm passed over, they were able to escape to safety. In an interview ten years later, the owner proclaimed the oak, *A Tree of Life for those who clung onto it for hope.*[1]

Surely, Ovenia would be thrilled to know the wisdom of her decision that day, and proud as a parent to see her tiny sapling become a tree of life. Sadly, the mighty oak did not survive the fury of the storm. Smothered by debris, it died a hero's death. In later years, the survivors commissioned a sculptor, who masterfully transformed the dead wood into an angelic work of art featuring three angels. The tree now resides across from the restored inn and brings charm and a legacy of hope to all who visit.

The smallest decisions can yield the greatest results.

Additional information:
- The storm caused approximately 1,200 deaths after levees broke and flooded New Orleans. Its immense surge crushed coastal Mississippi and Alabama.

The Angel Oak

Oak trees rank among the most popular of trees, prized for their strength, longevity, and usefulness. This majestic tree stands as a symbol for all trees and holds the title of State Tree for New Jersey, Maryland, Illinois, Connecticut, Georgia, Iowa, and Washington, D.C.

Oaks come in many varieties and can be red or white, evergreen, or deciduous. Six hundred species exist worldwide with over ninety in the United States.[2] One can identify a specific oak by its leaf. The acorns they produce provide food for a variety of birds and other animals. When pounded into flour, the acorns make a nutritious bread used by Native Americans and people with allergies to white or wheat flour.

The Northern Red Oak, New Jersey's state tree, sends out branches of red wood and sports bright red leaves in the fall. The coarse grain provides a durable wood that works well in a variety of projects. Some of its uses include railroad ties, flooring, furniture, and fence posts.

Another famous tree, the Angel Oak, lives in South Carolina. Because it is one of the most popular oaks in the U.S., thousands visit Johns Island to marvel at the 400-year-old, sixty-five-foot tree. Its longest branch is 187 feet with a circumference of twenty-eight feet. This amazing tree provides shade that covers 17,200 square feet. What a delight on a hot day!

The Angel Oak inspires respect and awe while providing protection. In 1991, the community supported Charleston in the purchase of surrounding land to protect it from future development.

A tree of this magnitude keeps us humble. It serves as a reminder that we are but a small speck in a very large world. When seen from space, the tree's sprawling branches are like a warm embrace.

The Trees Shake Before the Wind

When the house of David was told, "Syria is in league with Ephraim," the heart of Ahaz and the heart of his people shook as the trees of the forest shake before the wind.
ISAIAH 7:2

Ahaz, the cowardly and evil king of Judah, was filled with wickedness, which included the sacrifice of his own son to the detestable god, Molech. (2 Kings 16:1-4)

Isaiah 7:2 tells us the heart of the king shook. And in that moment of fear, he had to trust God. Isaiah and his son brought this sovereign message to Ahaz: *Say to him, "Be careful, keep calm and don't be afraid. Do not lose heart because of these two smoldering stubs of firewood."* (verse 4)

Though Syria and Ephraim plotted the ruin of Ahaz, God had different plans.

Yet this is what the Sovereign LORD says: *"It will not take place; it will not happen ..."* (verse 7)

Verse 9b warns Ahaz, *"If you do not stand firm in your faith, you will not stand at all."*

This magnificent account of God's sovereignty goes on to tell a grander story: the destruction of these two kingdoms and the revelation of one who will last forever. It is the prophecy of the virgin birth of Christ: Immanuel—God with us.

We know from history the birth of Christ was the fulfillment of prophecy. This assures us of the certainty of future prophecy: Christ will return and establish an everlasting kingdom on earth where peace, justice, and truth will reign. This is hard to believe given the corruption of rulers and powers in the world as we know it. They leave us feeling defeated and hopeless.

The notion of powerlessness deeply affects our daily lives. It saps our strength and causes us not to expect more. But what you see is not always what you get. God remains in control and we have His power available when we engage the Holy Spirit who lives within us. *But I say, walk by the Spirit, and you will not gratify the desires of the flesh.* (Galatians 5:16)

God is the same yesterday, today and forever. Our job is to trust and keep our eyes focused on Him, not the world around us. Just as He showed wicked Ahaz the end of times, He assures us all will be well in the end. But it is necessary to understand we work in partnership with God and have an important part to play in our stories.

Faith is an active posture we assume when life gets hard. Many are the struggles that threaten to sap our strength, but God asks us to look at life through a different lens. Life is complex, but when we switch focus from our circumstances to God's will, we are confronted with a much different picture.

Reflections

1. How would your view change if you looked down from the top of a tree?

2. King Hezekiah is known as the good king of Judah. Do you know who his father was?

The shaken people of Judah were not God's people; they were really the people of King Ahaz. They were shaken and unstable. A heart moved, as trees swayed by the wind, is unstable in all things. Our world may be unstable, but God is not.

3. When you place your trust in God, you gain His peace. Who will you choose to follow and where will you choose to focus?

4. We must be on guard for unseen enemies. What unseen enemies might you face?

5. The surge from a storm can pose a greater potential for death than the hurricane itself. What life situations could this describe?

Your smallest decisions can yield the greatest results. Remember Ovenia's small sapling grew into the Angel Tree of Bay St. Louis. It is a physical reminder that hope brings rewards.

Chapter 2
Anne Frank

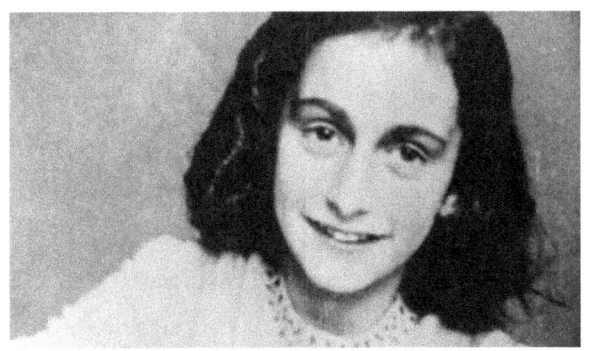

The Secret Annex

For there is hope for a tree,
if it be cut down, that it will sprout again,
and that its shoots will not cease.
JOB 14:7

Walking along, he stopped to admire the tree, a chestnut in full bloom. As his eyes traveled up the trunk to the great expanse of leaves, he spotted movement, not from within the tree, but from the backdrop of a warehouse, the warehouse where he worked. By the time he narrowed his gaze they were gone. But he was certain he spied a young girl and boy in the attic looking at the very same chestnut tree. Perhaps he would alert the authorities. The warehouse was closed today. No one should be inside . . . especially a young girl and boy.

No one knows for certain how Anne Frank and seven others hiding in a small apartment were discovered. Some believe they were betrayed by one of their helpers, but that is not proven. Could it be that a passerby spotted them . . . perhaps a worker, or his wife with whom he shared his sighting?

Anne Frank and her family went into hiding in July 1942. They hid in a secret annex successfully concealed by a bookcase for almost two years. They enjoyed no fresh air, no nature, no sunshine, no school, no other people, except those who sought refuge with them. The Franks were a family of four, joined by the Van Pels family of three, and Fritz Pfeffer, a Jewish dentist who came later. The group lived with the fear of discovery, as well as the onset of loneliness from never seeing, feeling, or interacting with the outside world.

In August 1944, an anonymous female voice phoned in a tip that led the authorities to their haven. All eight were captured and sent to various concentration camps. Seven met their death by starvation, disease, or gas chamber. Among them, were Anne and her sister. They were sent to a camp together where both died of typhus; first her sister Margot, then Anne two days later. Anne's father, Otto, was the only survivor.

What a sad and tragic end! How did eight people live in isolation for two years? They were under each other's feet, in each other's space, arguing, adhering to a strict schedule, fearful, anxious, uncertain. The record of Anne's diary and her other writings provide us details into a mystery that would otherwise remain unknown.

The timing alone is tragic. Anne received a diary for her thirteenth birthday and her family went into hiding one month later. Little did she know a few weeks after receiving the diary, her life experience would provide the richest material a stunned and saddened world would behold. In it she wrote, "I don't want to have lived in vain like most people. I want to be useful or bring enjoyment to all people, even those I've never met. I want to go on living even after my death!"

Anne died in a concentration camp of starvation and disease in February 1945, her body thrown into a mass grave. Just a few weeks later, on April 15, 1945, British forces rescued the captives and brought them to freedom. Lastly, if their hiding place had not been betrayed, Anne and her seven housemates would have walked out alive and free only six months later, when the war finally ended.

Her writings, filled with a hope-centered confidence, carried Anne Frank through a horrific experience. But it is from a tree that she received her nourishment and revival, a chestnut tree. She wrote, "As long as this exists, this sunshine and this cloudless sky, and as long as I can enjoy it, how can I be sad?"[3]

All the windows in their small apartment were blacked out to avoid detection. But Anne could still people watch, standing off to the side. That scene, however, could not compare to the uncovered attic window where a neighbor's chestnut tree filled the frame. It brought rejuvenation as she watched the life of birds, the movement of the sky, and the beauty of the heavens.

> *"I don't think of all the misery, but of the beauty that still remains."*
> *- Anne Frank*

Writing helped Anne sort through her physical, emotional, and spiritual observations as a teenager. But she cherished nature and found solace and nourishment in it, especially in the tree she wrote about several times in her diary. She marked the seasons, watched its growth, and dreamed a lifetime of dreams in the presence of the chestnut.

"The best remedy for those who are afraid, lonely, or unhappy is to go outside, somewhere where they can be quite alone with the heavens, nature, and God. Because only then does one feel that all is as it should be and that God wishes to see people happy, amidst the simple beauty of nature. As long as this exists, and it certainly always will, I know that then there will always be comfort for every sorrow, whatever the circumstances may be. And I firmly believe that nature brings solace in all troubles."

The Chestnut Tree

The chestnut, a deciduous tree, includes nine different species, but the two primary varieties are American and Chinese. Their bark is reddish-brown or grey and begins smooth, but becomes rough with age. They come from the same family as the oak tree. This makes the wood very durable for natural outdoor use. Chestnut trees produce many nuts that are flat, triangular, sweet, and good for eating.

The most impressive chestnut tree is named, Tree of One Hundred Horses. It lives in Sicily, Italy, on Mount Etna, considered one of the most active volcanoes in the world. This chestnut holds the Guinness World Record for the tree with the greatest girth ever.[4] And is numbered between 2,000-4,000 years old, which makes it the oldest chestnut tree in the world, surprising because the tree sits only five miles from the volcano's crater. Due to age, the tree is now in three pieces, but a look underground shows all three come from the same root.

The name, Tree of One Hundred Horses, came from a legend about the Queen of Aragon. Her company of 100 knights were caught in a severe thunderstorm during a trip to Mount Etna. They took refuge under this impressive tree and thus the name was born.

Anne Frank's famous tree however, is a horse chestnut, which is not a true chestnut tree. The nut it produces is round and all parts of the horse chestnut are poisonous to humans. But the flowers it produces between April and June are beautiful and uplifting. The clusters of pink or white flowers grow upright and measure five to twelve inches tall. The horse chestnut also has twisted limbs and interesting bark that exfoliates when it ages to reveal a beautiful orange color. It is no mystery this tree would delight and inspire Anne Frank.

"I want to go on living even after my death!"

She truly received her wish. Anne's diary serves as a legacy of hope for millions. A living legacy also exists to remind us of the beauty that still abounds. Her cherished chestnut tree lived to 150 years old, but grew diseased and weak.[5] More than half the tree was rotted because of fungus and insects. A steel support system was erected to uphold the rotted trunk.

When authorities spoke of removing it for public safety, people became enraged at the thought and a global campaign ensued to save the tree. A court reprieve was granted at the last moment. Despite their efforts, in 2010, the old tree behind the Secret Annex gave way. Battered by storm and wind, it fell to the ground taking its support with it.

But a new day has emerged, bringing hope and rebirth. From the original trunk came a shoot, pointing straight up to heaven. Seedlings have sprouted, original chestnuts collected and nurtured, and the "real" Anne Frank saplings are growing in museums, municipalities, schools, and other places.[6] These keep the story and hope of Anne Frank alive. Her chestnut lived a life of love, giving, controversy, and reward much like our journey. May we experience the hope in her words.

> *"I want to go on living even after my death!"*
> *- Anne Frank*

"I don't want to have lived in vain like most people. I want to be useful or bring enjoyment to all people, even those I've never met. I want to go on living even after my death!"

The Early Church

For by grace you have been saved through faith. And this is not your own doing; it is the gift of God, not a result of works, so that no one may boast.

EPHESIANS 2:8-9

The oppression that separated Anne and the others from general society is not new to history. Between 1933 and 1945, six million European Jews along with millions of other imperfect people, including the intellectually disabled, dissidents, Romanians, and homosexuals were shamelessly murdered under the direction of a madman. This was a time when all Jews were forced to wear a yellow star and banished from common areas. It was the culture Anne Frank last experienced as a free young woman.

Throughout the history of the church, Christians have experienced persecution. Among a few was Stephen, stoned to death and whom Paul addresses as his "true son in the faith." Likewise, Polycarp, an early Christian leader, and bishop of Smyrna, was burned at the stake, then stabbed when the fire did not kill him. Later an organized persecution of Christians ensued. Ancient historians blamed Nero for the Great Fire of Rome, but "Nero himself blamed a rebellious new cult—the Christians." Most modern historians do not blame Nero for the fire.[7]

The Apostle Paul was beheaded. The Apostle Peter was crucified upside down at his request, as tradition recounts, because he felt unworthy to die as Christ had. The Emperor Domitian persecuted Christians because of their association with the Jews. This is when the Apostle John was exiled to the Isle of Patmos and penned the book of Revelation.

Ignatius, a patriarch of Antioch was an early Christian writer and contemporary of Polycarp. Both were believed to be disciples of the Apostle John. Ignatius was brought to Rome by ten soldiers, to be killed by the lions. His own writings and later accounts state he was sport for the lions during the Colosseum games.

Today, persecution is rampant around the world, for Christians and anyone deemed unworthy by certain powerful enemies. Hatred is evil and we must guard against it.

The most famous martyr of all time, Jesus Christ of Nazareth, was crucified and died on the cross to atone for the sin of the world. In each of these cases life ended, but in the case of Christ, life began.

Martyrdom, the worse circumstance of all, did not defeat Christ. Rather it made an everlasting way of hope for us. Our worst current circumstances cannot stand against this truth: that life here is but a glimpse, and eternity is forever.

The resurrection of Christ is the heart of the Christian faith. Predicted first in the Old Testament, then by Christ Himself, this miracle, two thousand years ago, is the most authenticated event in history. The empty tomb is proof of His deity and guarantees the believer a future resurrection. It is done.

"It is finished." John 19:30, Jesus' final words tell us that the original sin of Adam, which separated us from God, is now and forever atoned.

"Where there's hope, there's life.
It fills us with fresh courage and makes us strong again."
- Anne Frank, *The Diary of a Young Girl*[8]

Reflections

From her only window to the outside world, Anne Frank could see the sky, birds, and a majestic chestnut tree.

"As long as this exists, how can I be sad? I don't think of all the misery, but of the beauty that still remains. Think of all the beauty still left around you and be happy."
- ANNE FRANK

1. Based on this quote, what can we learn from this young girl who saw beauty and life amid fear and death?

2. How does your thinking align with hers and how is it different? What changes can you make to look for the treasures in each day?

3. In what areas, do you see persecution today? Have you experienced persecution?

4. What types of prejudice exist today? Have you experienced prejudice?

5. What prejudices do you have? If you are uncertain ask God to reveal this to you.

Chapter 3
Sir Isaac Newton

A Great Thinker

*Set your minds on things that are above,
not on things that are on earth.*
COLOSSIANS 3:2

Could a blow to your head inspire a theory that would forever inform mankind? Many believe that is what happened to Sir Isaac Newton. They say while sitting beneath a tree, an apple struck him on the head, and caused him to ponder gravity. Though interesting, it is not completely true. But his life story, which does include an apple tree, offers insight into his genius.

Isaac Newton is best known for discovering the laws of gravity. As he watched an apple fall from a tree, (without hitting him on the head), he wondered many things: why the apple did not fall sideways or float upwards, how this force worked in the universe, why planets and the sun orbit, and why the greater the mass, the greater its pull.

Over his lifetime, Newton contributed to physics, mathematics, astronomy, literature, theology, optics, and calculus, but tolerated no criticism of his work. Insecurity perhaps led him to withhold some of his discoveries. As a result, rivalries erupted into lawsuits and arguments with other scientists who published before him, what he thought was his work. Both claimed the other stole their work. His traumatic childhood while causing him to withdraw and become a social pariah, paradoxically drove him to excel academically.

Newton was born prematurely in January 1643. Three months prior, his father suddenly died leaving his mother to raise him alone. She remarried a few years later, but her new husband, a pastor, had no interest in raising a stepson. Sadly, she made the heart-wrenching decision to abandon Isaac at age three, leaving him in the care of her parents. She went on to establish a new life and family that included three other children.

Losing his only parent at such a tender age and watching a new family replace him, left Isaac hurt and disoriented. A journal entry when he was 19 listing his sins, included "threatening to burn them and the house over them." He especially detested his stepfather.

He received a bachelor's degree from Trinity College at Cambridge University, just before the school closed for two years because of an outbreak of the bubonic plague. This forced him to return to his childhood home. And behold a tree . . . while sitting under an apple tree, he had the revelation of gravity and force.

The Flower of Kent Apple Tree

The Flower of Kent, first discovered in 1629 in Kent, England, produces a large apple, beneficial to the culinary world. The soft and sour texture dissolves into a puree when baked and is used to make a traditional English apple pie. This apple grew in the garden of Isaac Newton's childhood home, Woolsthorpe Manor, in 1660. Thus, the home became a popular stop for visitors who wanted to see the famed Flower of Kent Apple Tree.

A storm uprooted the tree in 1820, but many continued to visit the site, taking wood for trinkets, and making sketches to remember the original. Then a miracle occurred; out of the roots a new tree emerged.

The study of tree rings, dendrochronology, confirms by age that the tree is the original. And it holds the honor of being named among the 50 Great British Trees. The tree has branched out across the world, growing in spots that honor Newton's observations. Grafts were taken and sent to various locations prior to the regrowth. One of these is Trinity College at Cambridge, to honor Sir Isaac Newton's contribution to science and his association with the University.[9]

In 1727, this admired mathematician and physicist died. He was buried at Westminster Abbey. But the apple tree, made famous through his deep reflection, endures at Woolsthorpe Manor.

Sin

> *For all that is in the world—the desires of the flesh and the desires of the eyes and pride of life—is not from the Father, but is from the world. And the world is passing away along with its desires, but whoever does the will of God abides forever.*
> 1 JOHN 2:16-17

Isn't it interesting that the genesis of sin and the origin of physics both begin with an apple? Newton wrote more about biblical interpretation than he did about mathematics or science. However, he kept these writings private, possibly because they would be misunderstood or mislead others.

His nonscientific writings remained successfully hidden for a long time. But in 1936, two centuries later, they were discovered and auctioned. Years later the news outlets got wind of the discovery and he was accused of heresy and occult activity—the very thing he attempted to avoid.

Newton had a mind that was curious in all areas. He studied the Bible for weeks on end. Miracles, prophecy, dates, texts, and authorship were processed through the sieve of his great mind. His understanding of God's providence, reverence for his Creator, and examination of God's timeline are all evident in his writing.

Adam and Eve's original sin unleashed evil previously unknown into the world. From the beginning of time, man fell captive to his own selfishness and sin multiplied. Today, we see a fallen world and fiction presented as fact often with the media as willing accomplices.

In Newton's day, most of society still embraced a biblical worldview. Today, few restraints exist and the majority worship at the altar of relativism. Open-mindedness for every philosophy other than Christianity prevails.

Newton, the victim of media opinion would surely be mortified by their conclusions about his private theological questions. He does not deserve to have his great scientific contributions tainted by unfair conclusions about his spiritual life.

The books of Proverbs and Ecclesiastes say much about the fool of many words.

> *When words are many, sin is unavoidable,*
> *but he who restrains his lips is wise.*
> PROVERBS 10:19

> *The fool delights in shameful conduct,*
> *but a man of understanding has wisdom.*
> PROVERBS 10:23

A fool multiplies words, though no man knows what is to be, and who can tell him what will be after him?
ECCLESIASTES 10:14

The Bible was Newton's primary authority on God. In one manuscript titled, *Rules on Interpreting Prophecy*, he commented that simplicity and unity were common goals for both the scientist and prophetic researcher. He even spoke against the "folly of interpreters who foretell times and things by prophecy."[10] Below are some quotes from his writing. We should allow his own words to reveal the heart of this great man.

"This most beautiful system of the sun, planets, and comets, could only proceed from the counsel and dominion of an intelligent and powerful Being… This Being governs all things, not as the soul of the world, but as Lord over all; and on account of his dominion, he is wont, to be called Lord God."[11]

"We account the Scriptures of God to be the most sublime philosophy. I find more sure marks of authenticity in the Bible than in any profane history whatever."[12]

"When I wrote my treatise about our system, I had an eye upon such principles as might work with considering men for the belief of a Deity, and nothing can rejoice me more than to find it useful for that purpose."

On interpreting Scripture: "It is the perfection of all God's works that they are done with the greatest simplicity … And therefore, as they that would understand the frame of the world must endeavor to reduce their knowledge [science] to all possible simplicity, so it must be in seeking to understand these [prophetic] visions."

"The true God is a living, intelligent and powerful Being … He governs all things, and knows all things that are or can be done."

In his own words, Isaac Newton reveals himself to be a believer in orthodox biblical truth. Unfortunately, society has come to equate a biblical worldview with quackery. Newton is an excellent example of the compatibility of science and biblical truth. When science disagrees with the Bible, a believer knows at some point it will be proven wrong. The Maker of the universe knows all truth and will lead all those with receptive hearts into that truth.

He who restrains his lips is wise.
Ecc. 10:14b

Reflections

1. List some verses from Proverbs or Ecclesiastes about the "fool."

2. How can early trauma affect decisions today?

3. In what areas are science and biblical truth compatible?

4. Isaac Newton made a list of his sins. Can you make a list of yours?

Chapter 4
Joyce Kilmer

I Think That I May Never See

Joyce Kilmer shone as a journalist, lecturer, literary critic, and war hero, but was best known for writing the famous poem, "Trees." A little-known fact about this poet is that Joyce is actually a male. Named after two priests, Alfred and Joyce, at the Episcopalian Church where he worshipped, Kilmer chose to primarily use his middle name Joyce, to honor the priest who baptized him.

When he wrote the poem "Trees," Kilmer worked from a second-story office—also his bedroom—in Mahwah, NJ. His scenic view included a variety of saplings and fully grown trees: oaks, maples, and both white and black birches. Some institutions claim he wrote about a specific tree in his poem, but according to his son, he had the beauty and awe of all trees in mind.[13] This makes sense given the wooded landscape he looked down upon. His appreciation of nature coupled with his faith in God inspired his writings.

Kilmer lived a life of faith, in the shadow of much family death. He was the youngest of four children born to his parents, Frederick and Annie, whose second and third born children died after one year of life. He loved and admired his older brother Andy. Then sadly, Andy took his own life at the age of 26. Kilmer was only 13 years old and from then on, his parents clung to their only living child.

Marriage did not exempt Kilmer from the sting of death. He and his wife had five children. His second child, a daughter named Rose, tragically suffered from polio, causing infant paralysis. She lived only five years. A distressed Kilmer found solace through correspondence with a Catholic priest and later converted to Catholicism.

Kilmer wrote that he, "believed in the Catholic position, the Catholic view of ethics and aesthetics, for a long time," and he "wanted something not intellectual, some conviction not mental—in fact I wanted Faith." Kilmer would stop "every morning for months" on his way "to the office and prayed for faith," claiming that when "faith did come, it came, I think, by way of my little paralyzed daughter. Her lifeless hands led me; I think her tiny feet know beautiful paths. You understand this and it gives me a selfish pleasure to write it down."[14, 15]

His daughter died a few months before Kilmer was deployed to Europe, during WWI. At that time, he was considered the leading American Roman Catholic poet and lecturer of his time. While enlisted, he was able to hold an officer's position, but refused saying he would rather be a sergeant and part of the fighting brigade.[16] He put himself at risk choosing the most dangerous assignments. And he was killed on mission by a sniper shot, after joining a battalion to lead the attack of the day.

Alfred Joyce Kilmer (1886-1918) died at age 31, leaving behind his wife and four remaining children. This devastated his parents, who now lost their last living child.

Many tributes and memorials exist in his honor. One notable memorial is a hiking trail through the National Forest in North Carolina, a living tribute to honor his service as a veteran and his contribution as a poet. In an attempt to curb logging, the federal government preserved and dedicated 3,800 acres of trees to the memory and service of Kilmer.[17] The memorial forest accommodates a two-mile hiking trail in the shape of a figure eight or infinity symbol. "Trees" will live endlessly for generations to come.

Poplar Cove

The Joyce Kilmer Memorial Forest displays over 100 varieties of trees including many over 400 years old. Of the magnificent natural sites in the United States, this forest would rank high as a first-growth forest. This type of forest has experienced little disturbance, which results in older trees and ecological features that are exceptional and distinctive. Never logged, the forest ecosystem offers primitive charm with native trees that naturally regenerate and a diverse wildlife population.

In the 3,800-acre forest, trees grow to 100 feet high, some with a circumference of more than 20 feet around. What a fitting tribute to Joyce Kilmer who found refreshment in nature and wonder in the trees that God created. The upper loop of the infinity design of the hiking trail travels through a grove of the largest trees called Poplar Cove. The winding trail is a living memorial to Joyce Kilmer.[18]

The trees in Poplar Cove are the yellow poplar or tulip poplar, the largest tree in the eastern forest. In late May, tulip-like flowers sprout from the ends of the branches, high up in the tree, so high that you can only see it from a mountain or the top of another tree. For this reason, they are also known as the tulip tree. They turn a deep shade of gold in the fall and are beautiful to behold.

Tulip poplars grow deep in well-irrigated and drained soils. When early settlers saw them, they knew they had prime farming land. They are too large for city landscapes or suburban homes.

Only God

And God said, "Let the earth sprout vegetation, plants yielding seed, and fruit trees bearing fruit in which is their seed, each according to its kind, on the earth." And it was so. GENESIS 1:11

He is like a tree planted by streams of water that yields its fruit in its season, and its leaf does not wither. In all that he does, he prospers.
PSALM 1:3

Trees
By Joyce Kilmer

I think that I shall never see
A poem lovely as a tree.
A tree whose hungry mouth is prest
Against the earth's sweet flowing breast;
A tree that looks at God all day,
And lifts her leafy arms to pray;
A tree that may in summer wear
A nest of robins in her hair;
Upon whose bosom snow has lain;
Who intimately lives with rain.
Poems are made by fools like me,
But only God can make a tree.[19]

Reflections

1. Take time today for a reflective walk among the trees. Note what you see, smell, hear, touch, and taste.

2. Did you know we also have two other senses? Vestibular is balance and a sense of movement; the awareness that you are moving when on an elevator. And proprioception, the awareness that parts of your body are moving and the pressure they apply.

Joyce Kilmer was inducted into the New Jersey Hall of Fame in 2019 for his poem "Trees." A park is named in his honor in New Brunswick, NJ, on Joyce Kilmer Avenue.

Chapter 5

Thomas Hardy

A Tender Embrace

*And as you wish that others
would do to you, do so to them.*
LUKE 6:31

Thomas Hardy, a Victorian poet and novelist, died at age 87. His was a life well lived, filled with accomplishments, but his writings and later his burial ritual, tell the story of a troubled mind. Imbued with political opinion and social injustice, both his prose and verse represent a struggle with passion and social division.

Educated by his mother in his early years, Hardy first attended school at the age of eight. He showed great academic aptitude throughout the years, but his family did not have the money to pay for a university education. So, his schooling ended at age 16 when he became the apprentice for an architect. He excelled in that field, enrolling in King's College London, and winning prizes for his work.

In his mid-twenties, Hardy was assigned to oversee the excavation of a graveyard. The churchyard at St. Pancras was set for destruction to make way for a new railroad terminal. He was not thrilled with this job as expressed in his poem, "The Levelled Churchyard." He speaks of a "jumbled patch of memorial stones," and the "piteous groans" the passengers should listen for. Those jumbled stones found their rest at the base of an ash tree. And the ash tree in turn protected them, as its roots grew in and around the gravestones like a welcoming embrace.

Thomas Hardy twice married, first to Emma for 38 years, and later to his secretary, Florence, who was 39 years younger than he. Florence was credited with seeing to his health and other needs, thus keeping him actively engaged with his writing. But his heart literally belonged to his first wife Emma.

Though estranged for 20 years, Hardy was devoted when Emma died. He took time out to revisit places where they met and fell in love, to the dismay of his second wife. His poetry reflects the "regret and remorse" he so deeply felt.[20] It is said to be the best poetry of his career.

After dictating his final poem to Florence, on his deathbed, Thomas Hardy contracted pleurisy and died a month later from a heart condition on January 11, 1928. His funeral at Westminster Abbey was contentious. Hardy wanted to be buried in the same grave as his first wife Emma. But his executor wanted him buried in the Poets' Corner at the Abbey. They reached a morbid compromise wherein his heart was buried with Emma and his ashes went to Poets' Corner.

Judging by his deeply sentimental poetry, novels, short stories, and last wishes, Thomas Hardy (June 2, 1840–January 11, 1928), would love the warm embrace of the ash tree's limbs around the gravestones he abhorred moving. Some of his notable works are *Tess of the d'Urbervilles*[21] and "The Levelled Churchyard."[22]

Excerpts from: The Levelled Churchyard

> "O passenger, pray list and catch,
> Our sighs and piteous groans,
> Half stifled in this jumbled patch
> Of wrenched memorial stones!
>
> We late-lamented, resting here,
> Are mixed to human jam,
> And each to each exclaims in fear,
> 'I know not which I am!'…
>
> …"From restorations of Thy fane,
> From smoothings of Thy sward,
> From zealous Churchmen's pick and plane,
> Deliver us O Lord! Amen!"[23]

The Ash Tree

More than 68 varieties of ash trees exist and 18 species are native to North America. They live from 150 to 200 years and grow between 30 to 115 feet high depending on the species. The majority are deciduous trees ranging from medium to large. Their wood is used to make baseball bats, tool handles, furniture, staircases, and some electric guitars.

Ash trees are common to residential landscapes. You can identify an ash tree by the diamond shapes in the bark and the helicopter seeds on the ground. They also have matched opposing branches and an airy canopy that lets the sun shine through. This allows flowers, like violets, to grow beneath. Ashes are a favorite nesting tree for nut hatches, woodpeckers, and owls.[24]

But ash trees are being attacked and devastated in large numbers by an invasive beetle named the Emerald Ash Borer. It is a green beetle from northeastern Asia that feeds on ash trees. The female beetle lays eggs in the cracks of the ash tree; the larvae feed under the bark until it grows to an adult in a year or two.

According to the U.S. Department of Agriculture, the beetle was found in the early 2000s living in several areas of the U.S. and was responsible for killing almost all the ash trees they infested. The good news is that the loss of forest canopy allows more sunlight to hit the ground where ash trees leave large quantities of seeds. And a critical tree produces a stream of seeds before it dies. So, saplings and seedlings are increasing!

Character

> *For man looks at the outward appearance,*
> *but the Lord looks at the heart.*
> 1 SAMUEL 16:7B

In his book titled *Woodlanders*, Hardy contrasts the character of a humble woodlander to that of a sophisticated socialite. He portrays a culture that values social status with all its advantages, over honesty and good character. It tells of the broken promise of a father for his daughter's hand in marriage and the allure of the world.

God does not assess people based on what our eyes see, our minds say, or our prejudices dictate. *For God does not show favoritism.* (Romans 2:11) He does not favor one person over another based on their wealth or fine appearance. God looks at the heart of man and honors the qualities of humility, love, and faithfulness. Our criteria are not His.

Even in judgement God does not show preferential treatment. *"Anyone who does wrong will be repaid for their wrongs, and there is no favoritism."* (Colossians 3:25) In James 2:1, He calls for believers to act accordingly in the church.

The Bible presents favoritism as an offense against God's commandment to love. James 2:8-9 instructs us, *"If you really keep the royal law found in Scripture, 'Love your neighbor as yourself,' you are doing right. But if you show favoritism, you sin and are convicted by the law as lawbreakers."* In Hardy's novel *Woodlanders*, the father who is an ambitious and vain man, showing no love, breaks his promise to Giles Melbury to marry the daughter and love of his life. The themes of broken promises, societal injustices, and moral compromise play out among the very trees where the woodlanders make their living.

Our Heavenly Father never breaks His promises. His character, exemplified in Christ, is our model for life. It is based on faithfulness to His Word. Faith is what separates us from the otherwise "good people" of the world. Yes, good deeds, kindness, and moral behavior set a civilization apart from pagan cultures. But the Bible says, *"Without faith it is impossible to please God."* (Hebrews 11:6)

When we think about our daily toils, there is a larger picture to consider. To what end do we accomplish our tasks? If only for this lifetime and perhaps a future legacy, the value is tremendously diminished, partly due to the erasing of history. However, when we view today from the standpoint of eternity with its rewards for believers and consequences for unbelievers, our focus changes from success, accomplishment, and personal reward, into a fervency to share true hope with our family and fellow man.

This larger view adds a depth of purpose to our days and vocation, successfully changing our focus from personal issues and desires, to a grander scheme on a grander scale. When we keep our focus on God's view, His plans and purposes, and remove our eyes from ourselves and our circumstances, we are rewarded with increased Christ-likeness; we increasingly reflect His image and grow in godliness, faith, hope and joy. Colossians 3:2 reminds us: *Set your minds on things that are above, not on things that are on earth.* This is where faith and the promises of God intersect.

Faith in God brings eternal value to our purposes today.

Reflections

> *Blessed is the one who trusts in the LORD, whose confidence is in him. They will be like a tree planted by the water that sends out its roots by the stream. It does not fear when heat comes; its leaves are always green. It has no worries in a year of drought and never fails to bear fruit.*
> JEREMIAH 17:7-8

1. Why does our first impression come from a person's outward appearance?

2. Write each phrase of this verse in your own words.

3. Write the definition that best fits the words trust and confidence from this verse.

4. How does that contrast with fear and worry?

5. What can you do to trust and not fear, have confidence and not worry?

Chapter 6
Betsy Ross

Fact or Lore?

Elizabeth Griscom Ross, also known as Betsy Ross known for making the American flag, was the eighth of seventeen children. She apprenticed for an upholsterer and there met her first husband. At the age of 21, she left Philadelphia, the home of her Quaker family and church, to elope with John Ross, which got her excommunicated from the Quaker Church. Together they opened an upholstery business, and during this time she sewed many flags.

Tragically, her first husband died in the military two years after their marriage. She remarried and her second husband was a sailor who was captured by the British at sea and charged with treason. His health failed and he died while in prison. She was married a third time, to a man she knew from childhood and who was also imprisoned with her second husband in Britain. She had seven daughters, two with her second husband and five with her third.

She and her daughters made flags, banners, and other items for the new nation after the Revolutionary War. In 1870, prior to the 1876 centennial, enthusiasm for the flag emerged. At that time, Betsy's grandson revealed how she sewed the first flag. The story he retold stated Betsy had a visit from General George Washington in 1776 with the design of a flag for the new nation. His design included a six-point star. But Betsy changed it to a five-point star so the cloth could be folded and the star made with one cut. At the time, others surfaced saying they had made the original flag, but her grandson's story confirmed Betsy created it.

Another piece of ancient folklore regarding Betsy is that she is buried in New Jersey under an oak tree. This is not just any oak. It is a giant oak tree located at a Presbyterian Church in Basking Ridge.

A historian named Kennedy found evidence after researching newspaper articles from 1901 and 1902, where she found villagers who said Ross was buried there and not in Philadelphia, but her tombstone had been stolen. In an archived speech given at the church's cemetery for the 1876 centennial, the most compelling evidence was found. The historian found words spoken by an E. M. Pennington who said, "Here lies the woman who made the first banner containing the stars and stripes after that honored old ensign had been adopted June 14, 1777."[25]

Other sources report that Betsy Ross, born in Philadelphia, was buried there also and her remains moved twice. These sources state she and her husband were relocated to The Betsy Ross Complex.[26] Oddly enough, a 2012 Betsy Ross website has the following comment: "Later the city had Betsy moved to the courtyard of the Betsy Ross house in 1975. However, workers found no remains under her burial site."[27]

We will never know for certain, since media and myth hold the same reliability. Thankfully, my interest is in the giant oak.

The Great White Oak—Gone But Not Forgotten

In April 2017, Basking Ridge lost its beloved Great White Oak (1417-2017). Believed to be the oldest tree in the United States, it proudly stood in the center of town next to an historic Presbyterian Church. Estimated at 600 years old, the tree showed signs of decline in leaf color, texture, and population over the past few years.

Oak trees can live up to 350 years, but this mighty oak lived on perhaps because the church became its anchor. As its massive branches grew throughout the years, the church built in 1717 could not have kept a more beautiful adornment. It is a miracle that it lived another 300 years.

Honored with logos, weddings, and countless photos,

perhaps the greatest hug came from school children connecting hands to see how many could fit around the massive trunk. As the regal symbol brought life to the area, it received great press. Not so for The Devil Tree (next chapter), another famous oak that stands close by.

The Great White Oak also receives great love and care. More than a century ago, the tree showed signs of decline. People sprang into action, going to great lengths to prop it up. Though this beautiful specimen is gone it will be remembered. And who knows . . . a shoot may grow out of the stump one day.

What Is Truth?

> *Therefore, Pilate said to Him, "So You are a king?"*
> *Jesus answered, "You say correctly that I am a king. For this purpose, I have been born, and for this I have come into the world: to testify to the truth. Everyone who is of the truth listens to My voice."*
> *Pilate said to Him, "What is truth?" And after saying this, he came out again to the Jews and said to them, "I find no grounds at all for charges in His case."*
> JOHN 18:37-38

Yet they crucified Him anyway . . .

Truth - "A verified or indisputable fact, proposition, principle, or the like." (Dictionary.com)

Fact - Jesus died by crucifixion at the hands of the Roman government.

Lore - "Collective knowledge or wisdom on a particular subject, especially of a traditional nature." (Dictionary.com)

Relativism - "The theory, especially in ethics or aesthetics, that conceptions of truth and moral values are not absolute but are relative to the persons or groups holding them." (Wordnik online)

Relativism has been embraced by much of society for the last hundred years. In contrast to relativism, Christianity is based on a standard of absolute truth.

Barna Research conducted a national survey on relativism versus absolute truth. Only 22% of adults believed in moral absolutes and 64% believed that moral truth was relative to each situation and based on feelings.[28] Tragically, when youth were polled only 6% believed there was an absolute moral standard they should live by.

Could this explain the confusion in our world?

Judges 21:25 relates a stark fact: *In those days there was no king in Israel; everyone did what was right in his own eyes.* Because Israel rejected their kings, they had no one to hold them accountable to obeying God's law, His standard. Left to their own devices and varying opinions, Israel fell into relativism and chaos resulted.

Reflections

1. What are the moral absolutes in which you believe?

2. Why does a culture need a leader?

3. What other areas need leaders?

4. How can you see that God is a God of order?

5. Who is the author of confusion?

6. Reflect on a shoot growing out of the stump. Read Isaiah 11:1. To whom does this refer?

Chapter 7
The Devil Tree

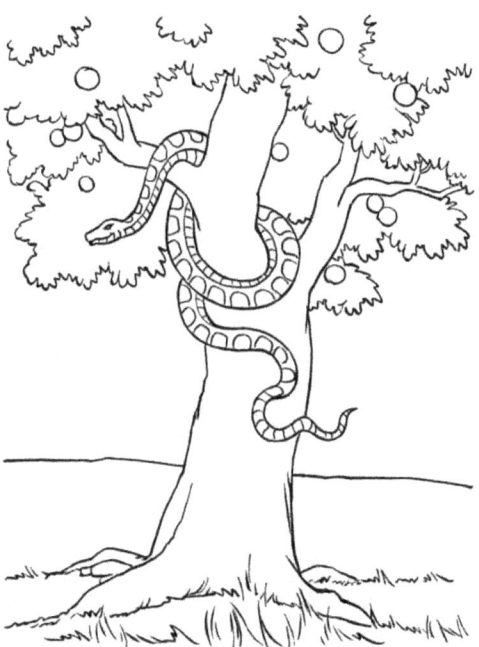

The fruit of the Tree of Knowledge was forbidden.

The Evil Twin

Good and evil siblings abound as central characters in many stories. Surprisingly, trees have the same associations. Two famous oaks reside in Somerset County, one of good repute, the other of ill-repute. Apparently, reputations even follow trees. And why not? They are living, breathing, contributing gifts of nature.

The previous chapter referenced the renowned Betsy Ross Oak. This is the "good" oak tree that beautifies the grounds of the Presbyterian Church of Basking Ridge. Many people do not realize it has an evil twin on Mountain Road named The Devil Tree.

The Devil Tree has grown in notoriety over the years. Gruesome stories abound including both past and present happenings. One such story tells of a farmer who killed his wife and children, then hanged himself on the tree. The tree had a long-extended limb that was rumored as a hanging spot for the KKK.[29]

Mystery and curiosity draw people from far and near to test its power. Some report hearing voices coming from the tree, others say it bleeds red, and some tell of seeing a ghost hanging from the tree. Teens are captivated by the mystery of the tree, filming it, and telling their own stories of intrigue. A mysterious truck with bright lights is said to have chased people away. And if someone dared to touch the tree, the superstitious believe something bad would happen to them.

Because of these stories, The Devil Tree is believed by many to be cursed.[30] Reports claim that it is a portal to hell and others testify that snow will not even collect at the base, because of the heat of hell.

The tree has been scarred over the years by attempts to burn or cut it down, resulting in a sinister appearance. Because of stories saying it bleeds red sap when cut, its dark, twisted, trunk is covered with many cuts and bruises that hinder the flow of sap to its upper limbs.

As homes are built closer and closer, the tree responds by looking tired and infiltrated. Although it stands in a valley all alone, the extended limb was removed for fear it would fall and injure someone. The area where the tree stands has been dedicated as a park. A chain-link fence encloses it and patrols protect it from vandals.

Trees Versus Stars

Do you believe there are more trees on Earth than stars in the Milky Way galaxy?

Scientists launched a massive effort to count trees—suspecting government records were wrong—due to their CO_2 calculations. Scientists were right. Using three sources: satellite, global volunteer counters, and natural resource directories, they found Earth was home to three trillion trees—eight times more than formerly believed. Surprisingly, the government figures were incorrect.

When astronomers worked to determine the number of stars in our galaxy, they explored using independent methods that included observing galaxy rotation, using spectral analysis, or examining past research data: some mathematical, some quantum. Naturally, their disparate methods yielded far different results. But for our purposes, the differences make no difference at all. Their calculations vary from 100-400 billion stars in the Milky Way galaxy.

Find out how they arrived at the numbers.[31]

If there are 100-400 billion stars to approximately 3 trillion trees, then there are 420 trees per person, but only 50 stars per person.[32] And approximately eight trees for every star.

Conclusion: There ARE more trees on Earth than stars in the Milky Way galaxy.

Trees in the Bible

He who has an ear, let him hear what the Spirit says to the churches. To the one who conquers I will grant to eat of the tree of life, which is in the paradise of God.
REVELATIONS 2:7 (ESV)

Interestingly, the Bible has a great deal to say about trees. Trees are mentioned more than any living thing in the Bible, excluding God and man. They bookend the entire text.

The very first chapter of the Bible mentions trees. *Then God said, "Let the land produce vegetation: seed-bearing plants and trees on the land that bear fruit with seed in it, according to their various kinds."* (Genesis 1:11)

Similarly, the last chapter mentions a tree. *On each side of the river stood the tree of life, bearing twelve crops of fruit, yielding its fruit every month. And the leaves of the tree are for the healing of the nations.* (Revelation 22:2)

Additionally, the very middle of the Bible mentions a tree. *That person is like a tree planted by streams of water, which yields its fruit in season and whose leaf does not wither—whatever they do prospers.* (Psalms 1:3)

Proverbs 3:18 refers to the Tree of Life, which is a reference to the Word of God, the ultimate source of wisdom. *Wis-*

dom is a tree of life to those who embrace her, and happy are those who hold her tightly.

Trees always reach upward seeking light. Likewise, every person of faith seeks light by looking upward. God's light provides guidance, wisdom, and encouragement. In John 8:12 Jesus says, *"I am the light of the world. Whoever follows me will never walk in darkness, but will have the light of life."*

What is the light of life? It is a life full of physical and spiritual blessing. Jesus is the likeness of the invisible God, Colossians 1:15, which means He is the light that shows us who God is. And the Holy Spirit gives us inner light or understanding of the Word of God and His will. Eternal life is synonymous with eternal light, earned for us through Jesus' life, death, and resurrection. Thus, light is the divine life made available to us through Christ's sacrifice. This divine life brings contentment and a deep inner peace.

The absence of light is darkness, the condition of man apart from God. This is different from the tendency of some to succumb to the burdens of the world, thus falling into depression and despair. Many believers have experienced the *dark night of the soul,*[33] a time of agonizing soul-searching or crisis of faith. Often this distress comes about as a reaction to the pressures and challenges of life.

As with all earthly challenges, God's answer is to lift our eyes away from our circumstances, and turn them upward to receive His light. Time with Him changes our perspective from self-focus to God-focus, which inevitably draws us outward to live like Jesus, to be His hands and feet and to share His light with others.

Perfect peace is found in God's perfect perspective. *You will keep in perfect peace all who trust in you, all whose thoughts are fixed on you.* (Isaiah 26:3)

Every good tree bears good fruit, but a bad tree bears bad fruit. (Matthew 7:17) Good trees seek the light and they produce good fruit for the edification of others. Bad trees turn inward toward darkness and rot from the inside out. Similarly, an inward focus often leads to sickness and suffering, and all selfish pursuits lead to the rotting of our souls.

We can be mirrors that brightly reflect the glory of the Lord.

Let us not only seek light like the trees, but also reflect it to others. *We can be mirrors that brightly reflect the glory of the Lord. And as the Spirit of the Lord works within us, we become more and more like him.* 2 Corinthians 3:18 (TLB)

Reflections

1. Reflect on God's creation. What thoughts come to mind?

2. Why did God give us trees?

3. What senses are stimulated when you look into the sky?

4. Take some time out to really look at a tree. Describe what you see and feel.

5. How does bright sunlight make you feel different from the darkness of night?

Chapter 8
The Belvidere Shoe Tree

Belvidere Shoe Tree

Then he said, "Do not come near; take your sandals off your feet, for the place on which you are standing is holy ground."
EXODUS 3:5

You could tell who the rich kids were on the island because they wore shoes. That is what my mom used to tell me about growing up in Trinidad, West Indies. And it was important to mom that her kids did not appear poor. So, she made sure they had shoes to wear to school. Amusingly, my sister relays a story about how when walking to school, my older siblings would remove their shoes and hide them in the bushes, because no one else wore shoes and they did not want to be different. Mother would be horrified if she knew.

Shoes have long signified wealth or status. And for many, shoes are primarily a fashion statement. Whether they are women's red-soled Louboutins, Jordan or Dior sneakers for teens, or men's Testoni shoes, footwear is used to make a statement. Because heeled shoes were worn primarily by men for riding horses because it kept their feet in the stirrups, heels came to signify a person's social standing or wealth.

In a similar shift, Audrey Hepburn brought loafers, a common men's shoe, into style for women when she wore them in the movie, *Funny Face*.[34] Today the average American woman is said to own over 34 pairs of shoes. This is nothing compared to the 749 pairs owned by Imelda Marcos, the First Lady of the Philippines from 1965 to 1986.[35]

Trees play a part both in the production and the preservation of shoes. A manufacturer named Allbirds developed a line of tree shoes made from the fibers of a eucalyptus tree. Wearers say they are fashionably comfortable. Anyone wishing to preserve their shoes employs a shoe tree. The best ones are made using raw cedarwood and are shaped like a foot. They easily slide into a shoe and preserve the life of the shoe.

In Belvidere, New Jersey, there stands the affectionately named Shoe Tree. To keep their shoes in the best condition, the local farming families would walk barefoot or in work shoes almost all the way to church, then pause at the Shoe Tree, put their Sunday shoes on, and proceed to the worship service.

A look at the tree today shows many shoes hanging from its limbs. Perhaps as a reminder of their history, or as a childish prank, people would throw their strung-together shoes straight up for the tree to catch. And there they remain as a token of times past. This white oak, one of the largest in the area, has a circumference of 15 feet and is around 350 years old.

As the community grew and the population increased, plans were made to widen the street next to the tree. The Shoe Tree would then need to be removed. But the residents protested and the tree was saved. Today it stands proudly in the middle of the road so drivers need to pay attention and not drive into it. The tree looks misplaced to those who pass through, but is a reminder to future generations of those who farmed the lands.

A Sappy Solution

Through nature God has provided food, medicine, wonder, beauty, and restoration. Through trees He literally provided the air we breathe. Trees are the lungs of the earth. They absorb carbon dioxide and release oxygen back into the air. We expel carbon dioxide and breathe in oxygen. It is a symbiotic relationship. The pine tree provides excellent examples of God's provisions. The lifeblood of a pine tree, the sap, is used for a multitude of practical and medicinal purposes.

In the past, not everyone had shoes or the money to fix them. When their shoes or work boots wore out, farmers would make a tar or resin from pine sap to repair their shoes. Some would even dip the bottom of their feet in the warmed pine resin and step in a bucket of sand. This became their shoes when they could not afford new ones. They repeated this process daily to protect their feet while working the fields.

The sap from a pine tree also has healing properties. The tree uses its sap to seal up any damage that occurs to its trunk. Likewise, the sap seals up human wounds like a stitch, and hinders the growth of bacteria. When mixed with ash and oil it becomes a treatment for skin rashes and irritations. When chewed it soothes a sore throat.

Pine sap is also an important survival tool providing first aid for cuts and bruises, a source to burn for heat, a natural insect repellent, and a torch for light. Mixed with charcoal from a fire, melted resin becomes glue. It can repair holes in a tent, seal up a drinking can, be shaped into fishhooks, harden tools, and waterproof items.

Native Americans used pine sap for stomach ailments and other medical conditions like arthritis. They would make a gum to chew or a liquid to drink.

As we behold the trees, let us remember what a gift from God they are, and the many blessings we reap from them.

New Shoes Please

For forty years I led you through the wilderness,
yet your clothes and sandals did not wear out.
DEUTERONOMY 29:5

Every day for forty years? Some things that we see as a curse, are really a miracle of God when we consider the whole picture. Most people would not even think about wearing the same shoes for ten years, yet the Israelites wore theirs for forty years.

Our culture values fashion, change and sparkle. We look at the trends and times to dress accordingly. When I think about how bathing suits have gone from one extreme to the other, I see the need to adjust. In centuries past, to bathe in the ocean women modestly covered up from head to toe. They wore so much clothing the joke was either bring a man with you or drown. Today some women wear so little, bathing suits look the same as undergarments.

Both are extreme, as is wearing shoes for forty years.

God is our provider. Yet sometimes we are discontent with His provision. We want more and better. Is that so wrong? Two schools of thought dominate the mainstream. One is that we should have everything we want. The other is we should deny ourselves everything. Once again, both are extreme. God gave us life to live and to live abundantly. But we are to be modest and temperate, sharing with others and not hoarding goods for only ourselves.

James 1:17 says, *Every good gift and every perfect gift is from above, coming down from the Father of lights, with whom there is no variation or shadow due to change.*

The fact is that we are all subject to unique differences and weaknesses. A temptation for you may not be one for me. So, we remain close to God, understand our personal challenges, and work to discipline ourselves through them. We are not entitled to have everything we may want. And we are not called to struggle in areas where we have means.

Our calling is to do good to all people. Galatians 6:10 instructs, *As we have opportunity, let us do good to everyone, and especially to those who are of the household of faith.* The idea is to get out of our own heads and desires. We are a selfish people by default, but God wants us to be a self-less people—looking to the needs of others, focused on obedience to Him, serving and carefully watching how we walk, so as not to be a stumbling block to another.

Excess and scarcity are poor examples of our calling. When we know who we are and whose we are, we will walk in a manner worthy of the calling of God. Paul admonishes us to do so in Ephesians 4:1. That means not focusing on ourselves, and living a life of joy and balance in the everyday common areas.

God understands our challenges.

Our extremities are important. Wear the shoes you want, but walk in obedience. Use your hands to worship and serve, to cleanse and rejoice, not to hold onto insignificant things that will become idols: a thought process, a horrible event, or a material thing. God wants your entire mind and heart devoted to Him. And when you do, the abundance of wealth equals more shoes than you will ever own.

Reflections

1. In what ways has God provided for you?

2. Recall a time when God's provision was amazing and unbelievable.

3. Explain why we are discontent at times and yearning for more?

4. What personal challenges do you face when it comes to possessions?

Chapter 9
Paul Smith College

The Leaning Pine

We are hard pressed on every side, but not crushed;
perplexed, but not in despair,
persecuted, but not abandoned;
struck down, but not destroyed.
2 CORINTHIANS 4:8-9

How far could you lean to one side before you fell over? A special pine tree, the pride of Paul Smith College, appears to defy gravity: It has leaned at what seems to be an impossible angle for almost 300 years. Located in New York's Adirondack State Park, the Leaning Pine remained slanted near the edge of St. Regis Lake for all those years.

Some attribute the angle to an accident of nature, but folklore tells a different story. Apparently, a hunting guide having overindulged in drink one night, found himself resting for the night on a sapling pine. Too young to hold the man's weight, the pine leaned over enough to provide him a comfortable spot for the night.[36] The pine's roots were strong and deep, having gained nourishment from the lake. With no attempt to straighten it out, it grew to 125 feet with no regard to direction.

The odd tree became the symbol for the college resulting in countless photos and artists' renderings of its unusual stance. The official symbol is the original drawing of a forestry student. Set in the wooded Adirondack Mountains, Paul Smith College offers a thriving forestry program. Unfortunately, in 1971, the perfect storm struck and three factors led to the leaning pine's demise. The quest for excellence in forestry education, an immature student, and an ill-prepared axe all conspired against the tree.

As part of the final exam, the condition of students' tools was inspected to ensure proper maintenance. To demonstrate good stewardship and respect for the forestry standards, students worked diligently preparing for a good grade. One student displeased because his dull axe resulted in a low grade, did the unthinkable. He took his anger at the instructor out on the pine, giving it several whacks with his axe. But still his wrath was not satisfied.

After a visit to the bar and in a drunken state, he and a fellow student took a chainsaw and proceeded to cut down the beloved tree. This occurred at 2:00 a.m. on November 11, 1971. Unfortunately, this outburst had a significant effect on the college's legacy.

Some reports claim fellow students cheered on the vandals. Others say more than the two students were involved in the crime. Nonetheless, when daylight came both campus and community mourned the loss of their leaning pine. Students passed with heads hung low in remembrance, some taking branches as keepsakes.[37]

A portion of the trunk now hangs as a tribute in the school's library. And the original sketch remains as a symbol on college grounds. In a poem about the tree, the poet concludes, "What took years to bring about, thoughtless man has again wiped out."[38]

The White Pine

The Eastern White Pine is the State Tree of Michigan and Maine and the provincial tree of Ontario. It can live for over 200 years and likes a cool, humid climate. It is not particular about its soil. Compared to other trees it is a fast grower and can reach 150 feet and over three feet in diameter. This makes it the largest conifer in the eastern forests. White pine is an evergreen that grows needles in clusters of five. Each grows three to five inches long and can produce both male and female pinecones during May and June.

The lumber it provides is useful because of its straight trunk and size. The Royal Navy, once the strongest navy in the world, used white pine to make their ships. The wood is durable, light, and stains to a beautiful finish. White pine is used for construction, millwork, trim, and pulpwood. It is good for paneling, doors, moldings, and trim work.

Additionally, the white pine has aesthetic and practical uses. It is a common Christmas tree because of its beautiful cone-like shape. Although, it is not ideal for hanging ornaments, it is impressive when lit and wrapped with garland. Not only does the tree provide shelter, but porcupine, deer, and songbirds feed on the seeds.

When food was scarce, the inner bark of the white pine was a food source for Native Americans. The Iroquois mixed the resin with beeswax to waterproof their canoes. The boiled bark was used in the healing of wounds and as a cough suppressant.

Unfortunately, it is a common allergen; the tree releases pollen that causes allergic reactions. But the white pine is another of God's creations that provides untold benefits for mankind.

Justice for the Pine

Do justice, love kindness, and walk humbly with your God.
MICAH 6:8

The attack described earlier in this chapter, was not the first attack on the oddly leaning pine at Paul Smith College. It is a reminder that some tend to attack anyone or anything that is different. The victim may be a bullied child, a disabled person, or an innocent tree. The college students involved were old enough to know better, but nevertheless they lashed out in malice.

On a prior occasion, the tree was attacked by other angry students. Workers used concrete to fill the damaged 38" trunk. So, when the tree cutting incident occurred, dorms were checked for axes damaged by the concrete. At that time, the culprits were not found. Months later, the very student who received the bad grade came forward and confessed to chopping it down. He and another student paid the fine of twenty-five dollars.[39] A twenty-five dollar fine does not seem fair punishment for the damage that was done. Years of disheartened students and alumni still feel the effect of the loss.

Bullying or marginalizing others is more commonplace than it should be. Many people struggle in adulthood because they were bullied as children. We cannot allow our past experiences to shape our lives negatively because like the leaning pine tree, God provides many ways for His unique people to compensate for and overcome the various challenges we encounter growing up.

God shows us the way to live victorious lives, not buried under the problems of life, but walking joyfully above them. Like Peter, when we keep our focus on Him, we can walk on water. He gives us the power to choose His way.

I choose to live victoriously. Yes, as many others, I have also been bullied, the odd person out, the different one, assaulted, abused, ignored, and discouraged. BUT I have victory in Christ and I live in that truth. It is my choice to move forward and make my life count for the Kingdom of God. The only thing of true importance is the future and our eternal home.

Right now, what counts are our motives, our present testimony, and our service to God. Since our focus determines our state of mind, rather than focusing on the past, let us do as the Apostle Paul recommends. . . . *Let us run with perseverance the race marked out for us, fixing our eyes on Jesus, the pioneer and perfecter of our faith.* (Hebrews 12:1b-2a)

Reflections

1. Have you been victimized by destruction?

2. When America lost the Twin Towers to terrorism, every citizen felt the loss. Have you felt the loss caused by someone else's destruction closer to home?

3. What have you suffered that challenges you to move forward?

4. What is required for you to move past pain, regret, and sorrow to forgiveness?

5. Loss causes grief. When we experience the five stages—denial, anger, bargaining, depression, and acceptance—we are on the road to healing.

Chapter 10
Methuselah

Methuselah—The Man

*When Enoch had lived 65 years,
he fathered Methuselah.*
GENESIS 5:21

Methuselah lived more years than anyone in history. The Bible tells us he lived to the age of 969. His name means Man of the Dart or Javelin. Back in Bible times, a few others lived into their 900s. Adam lived 930 years. His son Seth lived 912 years. Seth's son Enosh lived 905 years. Jered, Methuselah's grandfather, lived 962 years. And Noah, Methuselah's grandson, lived 950 years. Wow that is a long life!

I would not want to live that long. Life would get boring, ho hum, and I would long to be away from the evil in this world. They say there is nothing new under the sun, so the evil present today was surely present back then. That is a long time to deal with something.

Enoch provides another amazing example from Bible history. Known as a faithful man of God, he was Methuselah's father. The lyrics of the old hymn, In the Garden, "and he walked with me and he talked with me" remind me of Enoch. *Enoch walked closely with God. But then he was no more because God took him away.* (Genesis 5:24)

Methuselah died, not in the flood, but in the year of the great flood, when Noah was 600 years old. He would have seen the Ark built. What a heritage! Methuselah was the son of Enoch and the father of Lamech, who was the father of Noah.

The oldest living tree in history is named Methuselah.

The Bristlecone Pine

Almost 5,000 years old, Methuselah, a Great Basin Bristlecone Pine, still stands. In 2024 it was 4,856 years old. It is named after the biblical figure, Methuselah, who lived longer than any person in history. The tree lives in California, between the Sierra Nevada range and the Nevada border. The exact location is kept secret to protect it.

In 2013, another ancient pine in the same area was discovered. This one is even older, 5,073 years old in 2024. This tree's location is also kept secret for its protection.

How can trees live so long? It is unfortunate that once famous and known, things need to be hidden from the public for their safety.

Bristlecone pines grow at high elevations in isolated groves. They can withstand volcanic eruptions and ferocious storms to become more enduring than other trees. The dense, twisted trunk speaks of the harsh conditions they endure. They grow where nothing else will and sustain temperature shifts that would kill other trees.

Older cloned trees exist, like the Quaking Aspen or the Mojave Desert Creosote, but they were grown by taking roots from their original tree. The bristolcone pine is an original, not a cloned tree, making it even more special. Rooted in stone, and twisting its trunk for thousands of years, this tree has flourished through impossible conditions.

The Price of Fame

Mourn for her, all who live around her,
all who know her fame; say,
"How broken is the mighty scepter,
how broken the glorious staff!"
JEREMIAH 48:17

Let your eyes look directly forward,
and your gaze be straight before you.
Ponder the path of your feet;
then all your ways will be sure.
Do not swerve to the right or to the left;
turn your foot away from evil.
PROVERBS 4:25-27

If you heard the name Diana Frances Spencer, it might not ring familiar. But if you heard Princess Diana, a range of thoughts might cross your mind: first, a smile at the memory of a caring humanitarian, awe for the shy underdog who became a real princess and stirring thoughts of the castles, gowns, and princes some girls dreamt of as young children.

Eventually, thoughts of her tragic death would emerge, her short life, children left motherless, a demanding queen mother, and a neglectful husband. Finally, you would feel sadness for the heart of the woman who was thrown into the limelight: harassed by media, stalked by paparazzi, and having her poise admired while every move judged. She endured the loneliness of public life, without the comfort or counsel of a partner, but with the pity of the crowds, and fear of the future.

Do not swerve to the right or to the left; turn your foot away from evil.
Proverbs 4:27

The price of fame is a reminder that our path in life should be carefully weighed. We adore famous singers, artists, intellects, etc., but we cannot fully grasp the grueling schedules or scrutiny they endure from their "fans." Much good comes from the positive societal contributions of the rich and famous.

But there is a dark side. Often the famous pay a high price to realize their dreams and fill our world with music and hope. These include family loss, pride, fear of failure, and a continual compulsion to achieve more: power, attention, perfection, doing more, wanting more. Hollywood drug addiction is rampant. The rich and famous take pills to sleep and wake up. They hire doctors who travel with them, who are willing to violate their standards, just to be a part of their lifestyle.

Methuselah of the Bible lived a long and private life. He is mentioned only three times. Yet entire cults have come to elevate him as their god. "One of the most famous Methuselah cults, is centuries old."[40]

How then can we avoid supporting or even adopting an empty lifestyle? The Bible instructs us to *be careful when we stand, lest we fall.* (1 Corinthians 10:12) Instead, be vigilant because *the devil prowls around seeking who he can devour.* (1 Peter 5:8) We are called to guard against covetousness, envy, and greed.

As we walk uprightly, may we heed Paul's instructions to keep our eyes on the true prize, and run the race of life with perseverance; being careful to steward well the gifts we have received. May we live lives of gratitude and thankfulness for God's common and special grace in our lives daily. A life of self-examination before the God of the universe leads to untold riches and transformed lives.

Reflections

> *Therefore, since we are surrounded by so great a cloud of witnesses, let us also lay aside every weight, and sin which clings so closely, and let us run with endurance the race that is set before us, looking to Jesus, the founder and perfecter of our faith, who for the joy that was set before him endured the cross, despising the shame, and is seated at the right hand of the throne of God.*
> HEBREWS 12:1-2

1. Who represents the great cloud of witnesses in your life?

2. For what are you grateful?

3. What is the definition of perseverance? How well is it applied in your life?

4. Honest self-examination before God is fruitful. Have you evaluated your circumstances, thought life, routine? What things are most important to you?

5. In what areas requiring change do you struggle?

6. Can you relate to something being so precious that you must protect it? What do you keep hidden to protect it?

7. Do your daily activities reflect a relationship with God?

Chapter 11

The Hawaiian Kukui

Polynesia

Henry Obookiah

Henry Opukaha'ia, also known as Henry Obookiah, left Hawaii in 1808 on a merchant ship headed for the United States. As the first Hawaiian convert to Christianity, he trained to become a minister of the Gospel. He dreamed of introducing Christianity to the Hawaiian Islands. During his studies at a mission school in Connecticut, he shared stories of his homeland and the people, describing idol worship, and the victimization of his people by European sailors.

Unfortunately, Obookiah fell ill and died before he could carry the message of salvation back to his people. A bestselling memoir of his life deeply moved evangelical New Englanders who worked to realize his dream of bringing the hope of Christ to Hawaiians. Several of his classmates from the mission's school left Boston for Hawaii in 1819. After a trying five-month journey, seven couples finally saw the big island in the distance.

They were astounded at the remote tribal native people who met them almost naked. Although friendly and curious, to the dismay of the missionaries, the natives displayed no interest in learning to farm, sew, or cook. Even so, most of the couples stayed there for years opening schools and churches. They translated the Bible and other books into Hawaiian, and provided medical care.

In 2023, the New England Historical Society updated an article about Henry Obookiah.[41] It talks about the trauma he faced in early childhood having witnessed his parents tortured and killed, and his baby brother murdered by warriors who invaded the island. Obookiah was kidnapped and enslaved by the very warrior who murdered his parents. He lived with survivor's guilt because he was the only member of his family to survive the attack.

Obookiah was a descendant of a royal line of priests. One day his uncle, while traveling the island, found his nephew. As a kahuna-priest, his authority was higher than Obookiah's slave master. So, his uncle rescued him and trained him as a kahuna.

Obookiah would face many more crises. Some included seeing his aunt thrown off a cliff, fleeing Hawaii on a trade ship, and enduring the prejudice of people in Connecticut during slavery and segregation.

Among his blessings was converting to Christianity during the second Great Awakening in 1815, and meeting Harriet Beecher Stowe and her brother, Henry Ward. They later became abolitionists after being persuaded by Obookiah that all men are created equal.

In 1992, a campaign to bring Obookiah's body back to Hawaii succeeded. His remains are now buried in Kahikola Church Cemetery overlooking Kona's Kealakekua Bay.

The Kukui Tree

Although it originated in Polynesia, the Kukui tree represents the State of Hawaii. It is a tough tree that displays the beauty of silvery-green, maple-shaped leaves, white flowers, and green nuts. The trunk and branches, sometimes twisted, provide a great circle of shade. Related to the macadamia tree, the Kukui grows to almost 100 feet, and is also known as the candlenut tree.

Knowing its many benefits, early settlers brought the tree to Hawaii. To begin with, they were able to use the oily nuts as candles. Since these candles burned for 15 minutes, they utilized them to measure time. Pressed nuts produced an oil to burn in stone lamps. The leftover resin mixed with other matter made a cake that fertilized crops and fed cattle. The nuts also produced a dye used for tattoos. Roasted and chopped nuts made a delicious relish commonly served at luaus. The nuts are mildly toxic when raw, but added to broth they make a thick sauce.

Kukui nut shells and their delicate white blooms create the famous leis used to greet visitors to the island. From the flower, bees produce a sweet and unique Kukui honey. Kukui blooms are the official flower of Molokai. And leis made of Kukui nut shells are standard adornment at Hawaiian occasions. The nuts are usually sanded, buffed, and polished into various finishes, then laced with other adornment to make leis and bracelets.

Hawaiians attach much symbolism to the Kukui nut tree. It represents peace, protection, and enlightenment. Another use of the nuts has been as prayer tokens. And hula dancers, priests, and royalty all proudly wear them. Some couples exchange bracelets made from the shells during their wedding ceremony.

Finally, the buoyant trunks were made into canoes and painted with dye from the tree roots. Because of these numerous uses coupled with its rich history, unsurprisingly the Kukui candlenut tree won the hearts of Hawaiians and earned the title of Hawaii's State Tree.

The Yoke of Oppression

Whoever steals a man and sells him, and anyone found in possession of him, shall be put to death.
EXODUS 21:16

Slavery as we know it today was and is a crime of kidnapping, trickery, and captivity. From the African people, to young Asian girls, through innocent children worldwide, slavery is a product of evil. People taken against their wills, forced into the unspeakable, and treated as less than dogs is a disgraceful act of human cruelty.

But God sees all and His wrath is certain. *Woe to the world because of the things that cause people to stumble! Such things must come, but woe to the person through whom they come.* (Matthew 18:7) *It would be better for him to have a large millstone hung around his neck and to be drowned in the depths of the sea.* (Matthew 18:6b)

In the Old Testament, slavery was at times due to captivity, as in the Babylonian captivity of Israel. At other times, slavery included a range of situations and restrictions. But the Bible makes clear in Exodus 21:16 that capturing and selling people like chattel is a crime.

Slavery in the Old Testament was also an avenue for the poor to survive. They were able to work—giving them purpose, care for someone—giving them relationship, and collect pay—giving them some financial independence. They also entered slavery to pay off a debt, for protection, food, and shelter.

We know from Deuteronomy 15:4, that God's intention was not to see Israel poor. *But there will be no poor among you; for the Lord will bless you in the land that the Lord your God is giving you for an inheritance to possess.* He put several laws in place, found in Deuteronomy 24, to prevent slavery. But sin made it inevitable.

Another difference between captive slaves of today and yesterday was the opportunity for freedom. Slaves of the Old Testament could be set free after a set period, after a debt was paid, in the Year of Jubilee, or because they simply wanted to leave. A sad scene in the movie *Roots* was when Kunta Kinte was recaptured and they cut off part of his foot because he ran away.

Servanthood takes on a different meaning in the New Testament. Jesus called Himself a servant in Mark 10:45. *For even the Son of Man did not come to be served, but to serve, and to give His life as a ransom for many.* He is the greatest example of how we should live: Jesus was a servant leader. He came to do the will of God and serve His disciples, teaching and admonishing them. He does the same for us, to demonstrate a better way to live and to look at things, the way of humility. Slavery is hard to understand on any level. But Christ gives us these reassuring words to live by. May we follow His example.

Come to me, all who labor and are heavy laden, and I will give you rest. Take my yoke upon you, and learn from me, for I am gentle and lowly in heart, and you will find rest for your souls. For my yoke is easy, and my burden is light.
MATTHEW 11:28-30

Reflections

1. What various types of enslavement do we see today?

2. What differences/similarities do you see from biblical times to now?

3. What is a yoke?

4. What burdens are you carrying that require relief?

5. How does the example of Christ in Matthew 11 inform you?

6. What changes can you make?

When a person chooses sin, they are in bondage to that sin. Christ offers freedom from bondage to those who choose His way.

Chapter 12

The Tree of Life

Etz Chaim

When your words came, I ate them;
they were my joy and my heart's delight,
for I bear your name, LORD God Almighty.
JEREMIAH 15:16

Etz Chaim is a Jewish term that literally means the tree of life. It refers to the Tree of Life in the Garden of Eden, but also to the Bible as a tree of life to those who steward it well. Just as God created man, before the Garden and the trees, He also provided the Bible. It is His Word for man to feast upon and steward well. God gave us ways to grow healthy in mind, body, and spirit by giving us enjoyable work to fill our days, and the wisdom of His Word to fill our minds.

And the Lord God planted a garden in Eden, in the east, and there he put the man whom he had formed. And out of the ground the Lord God made to spring up every tree that is pleasant to the sight and good for food. The tree of life was in the midst of the garden, and the tree of the knowledge of good and evil.
GENESIS 2:8-9

The apple Eve ate did not come from the tree of life. It came from the other famous tree, the tree of the knowledge of good and evil. After the fall of man, God closed the Garden putting cherubim at the east end to guard the way to the tree of life. He did it so Adam and Eve would die and not live eternally under the curse of sin.

And the LORD God commanded the man, saying, "You may surely eat of every tree of the garden, but of the tree of the knowledge of good and evil you shall not eat, for in the day that you eat of it you shall surely die." (Genesis 2:16-17) Was this a test of Adam and Eve's obedience to God?

Then the LORD God said, "Behold, the man has become like one of us in knowing good and evil. Now, lest he reach out his hand and take also of the tree of life and eat, and live forever— therefore the LORD God sent him out from the garden of Eden to work the ground from which he was taken." (Genesis 3:22-23)

Sin changes us. The original sin of Adam and Eve changed their lives forever and it changes us today. Though we cannot escape sin we can fight it in the power of the Holy Spirit. God calls us to make choices. He arms us with spiritual weapons for the daily battles we face. He has placed the Holy Spirit within us to empower us to do what is right and convict us when we choose wrongly. But we need to take the first step.

God does not force His way into our lives or our world. He has given the world over to Satan, while providing a way of escape for His children. God in His mercy banished Adam and Eve, gave us a rainbow promise, left His living Word, sent Jesus to pay our debt, and instilled in us His Spirit. He desires an eternal relationship with us and has prepared an eternal home for those who follow Him. Will you?

The Balboa Tree

The Balboa tree, located in Madagascar and southern Africa, is fondly known there as the Tree of Life. It grows up to 100 feet, with a circumference of 165 feet and can live up to 3,000 years. It is known for being strong and resilient. The massive trunk stores water so these trees can survive in very dry areas. A few tales surround the odd-looking tree. Each story ends with the tree being tossed away upside down, explaining its unusual root-like head. In addition, the tree heals itself because its massive root system prevents soil erosion and recycles nutrients. It can grow new bark and its thick trunk makes it fire resistant.

The name Tree of Life is well deserved. In addition to the remarkable qualities listed above, the Balboa's bark and fruit have 300 essential uses. Its oval fruit can grow to a foot long and provides vitamin C and essential nutrients, nourishing humans as well. The tree waters and feeds elephants; its fruit delights baboons; while the nectar from its flowers provides delicious nourishment for storks, red-billed buffalo weavers and lemurs all who find protection by nesting in the tree. Every creature that feeds on the tree also fertilizes the ground with nutrient richness.

Man had to stop eating from the Tree of Life in the Garden of Eden. God did not intend humans to live immortally in a state of sin. Thus, man was cut off from the garden. When God brings down a new Heaven and Earth, we will again eat the twelve fruits of the tree.

Choose life.

The Apostle John wrote, *Blessed are those who do His commandments, that they may have the right to the tree of life, and may enter through the gates into the city.* (Revelation 22:14)

When God said, "You shall not eat." And yet they ate, their disobedience was the cause of their banishment. God provided Adam and Eve with many other trees for food. Yet they chose to disobey.

God gave a similar choice to Israel when He brought them out of Egypt. . . . *I have set before you life and death, blessing and curse. Therefore, choose life, that you and your offspring may live.* (Deuteronomy 30:19)

We have the same choice given to Adam and Eve and Israel. Today, we can choose life through a relationship with Jesus Christ or choose the world. One path leads to the knowledge of good and the other to the knowledge of evil.

Tree of Life Stories

I put a call out on Facebook for anyone who had a personal tree story. Here are a few I received.

Barbara Sako ~ My Refuge and Strength

Two trees, woven together, serve as a spiritual reminder that our Savior NEVER leaves us to fight our battles alone.

In the early 1990s I was diagnosed with Crohn's disease. By the time I saw a gastroenterologist the disease had progressed. This made it impossible for me to work and be the wife and mother I wanted to be. When I was told there was no cure, and colon removal was inevitable if all else failed, I was devastated. It was at that low point in my life, God directed me to II Samuel 22:31-37. *As for God, his way is perfect; the word of the LORD is flawless. He is a shield for all who take refuge in him. It is God who arms me with strength and makes my way perfect. You stoop down to make me great.* (Excerpts from Samuel 22: 31-3) I was pulled into the embrace of my Savior.

That afternoon, I hobbled outside and unexpectedly noticed two trees intimately fused together. The one on the front was stable and strong growing straight up toward the heavens for many years. It had been held all along by the tree behind it that stooped to support its growth. Wrapping its strong arms around the smaller tree, this servant tree offered its strength, providing refuge from the storms of life. It is a physical reminder of the love and protection of my Heavenly Father, a marvelous gift during my darkest days.

Joyce Livelli ~ The Avocado Pit

I always heard you could grow an avocado tree from a simple pit. So I took a pickle jar, filled it with water, and set the pit over the top; I propped it up with toothpicks and submerged the bottom in water. Then I waited . . . and waited . . . and waited.

After about six months, a crack appeared. Another month later, a little green stem poked out with some roots. After a year, a dainty leaf popped out. In six more months, I planted the sapling in dirt. It began to grow . . . really well! After a summer on the deck, it became an avocado tree.

The lesson here is that some seeds, like people, seem to grow quickly while others take love, nurturing and great patience. When they eventually sprout, they bring great joy well worth the wait.

Jennifer Prystash ~ The Mimosa Log

As a little girl, I loved my neighbor's mimosa tree. When it bloomed, I would bask in the fragrance for hours. The seeds that dropped grew into saplings. At age seven I planted one in my own backyard, placed a fence around it, and watered as needed. I nurtured the tree until it matured and bloomed on its own. I was so proud of my mimosa tree.

One sad day, my dad decided to build a garage right where my beautiful tree stood! I was sad because it was too big to transplant. After the inevitable removal, my dad saved a log-sized piece, and gave it to me when I left for college. When I got married and moved, the log came with me and is displayed proudly in my sitting room, where it continues to remind me of its inherent beauty.

Diane O'Brien ~ The Pear Tree

A pear tree that grew in my grandparents' yard was very special to me during childhood. Thoughts of it thrill my heart to this day, leaving me with a sense of intense love and safety. On a hot summer day, I could always find my grandparents sitting under its protective canopy. My aunts, uncles and cousins would gather on many Sundays for barbecues under the pear tree. The spreading branches offered welcome protection from the sun. I fondly remember how excited I became when my dad picked one of the delicious pears for me.

I am amazed by how trees draw us to God. Today I have a "prayer tree" right outside my window. I look at it every morning as I praise and thank God. A simple gaze draws me into the throne room of God and centers me as I pray; even in winter when it has no leaves!

Faith Craft ~ The Swinging Branch

One of my most disturbing memories is of the day my 84-year-old dad and my husband, Tom, decided to cut down a large tree. Dad held onto the rope they had tied around the tree's trunk to direct its fall. Unfortunately, when the tree began to tip, dad did not let go of the rope. It lifted him up and out and left him swinging over the side of a high cliff. Thankfully, it came back around and Tom was able to grab dad. Tom was especially grateful he did not have to explain what happened to me or mom. That ended the job for the day even though the tree never fell to the ground because it got caught in the branches of another tree. Dad commented, "The Lord would fell the tree." Within minutes a gust of wind came through and blew it down.

Deb Gatz ~ The Birch and The Spruce

When I was a young girl in coastal Maine, a hurricane came up the east coast and eventually reached our small town. The wind howled, the rain buffeted trees and buildings alike with unrelenting bucketfuls. The trees in our yard were blown first this way and then the other, looking as if they were participating in a magnificent tug-of-war game.

Two of our trees responded in opposite ways to the strong winds. One was a spruce tree and the other, a birch. After the storm, both trees showed some effects but one displayed more resilience than the other, which needed to be propped up.

The spruce tree was hit by lightning and was split from the top of the tree down to about 20-25 feet away from the bottom. The birch tree had multiple trunks that bowed down low in the wind, the tips brushing the grass during the more powerful gusts. I loved that tree and expected it to snap, but it just lay there, practically horizontal to the ground.

As soon as the storm abated, my dad climbed up the spruce tree with a length of rope to tie together the two halves of the tree hit by lightning. As the days passed after the storm, Dad would tighten the rope until he was satisfied that the spruce tree was safe to climb again. But the birch tree daily regained its strength, eventually standing tall and willowy, a reminder that flexibility can help us withstand the storms of life.

Beth Brubaker ~ A Lumberjack You Ain't

My dad's antics are a source of amusement for our family. He was not always the most ingenious problem solver but he meant well. He thought himself a "Jack of all trades," forgetting the adage ending, "master of none."

The huge pine next to our house constantly dumped its very long needles clogging the gutters of our home. Dad decided to solve the problem by cutting down this pine tree that grew between our house and the neighbor's house.

As usual, Dad sought directions, not in a book, but always in a "guy he knew." In this case the tree guy no longer lived nearby, so he shared his knowledge over the phone. Dad bought all the supplies he recommended and moved the car away from the driveway, where the tree was supposed to fall.

Dad hacked, chopped, and wedged but the tree would not budge. Then we heard a crack and ran! The tree bounced off the neighbor's power lines and landed next to the driveway. After a pause, Dad said, "Yep, that's exactly where I wanted it. And by the way, don't tell your mother." And to this day I never have.

Reflections

1. Do you have a true-life tree story?

2. How do you see God in it?

3. Reflect on God as you color in the picture.

Chapter 13
The Specialty of Three

The Three Trees

The Three Trees is a story about the hopes and dreams of three particular trees that stood together on a hilltop. Through the years they shared how they wanted to be used in the future. One wanted to become a treasure chest, the next wanted to be a ship that carried a mighty king, and the last wanted to become the tallest, straightest, and best renowned tree that pointed people to God as they looked upward at the branches.

For years they prayed, until one day woodcutters chose them. The first tree was cut and sold to a carpenter, the second to a shipyard, the third was taken with no purpose in mind. The first two trees were happy to see their dreams coming true. But the third was crushed. Being cut down put an end to his dreams of people communing with God in the heavens because of him.

None of the three would realize their dreams. The first was made into a feed box for animals, the second became a small fishing boat, and the third was chopped into large pieces and stored in the dark. Eventually all three forgot their early dreams.

Time passed when suddenly the feedbox was used to cradle a new baby. The first tree sensed the importance of the event and knew it held the greatest treasure of all time. Years later, the fishing boat encountered a storm it could not withstand until a sleeping man commanded the storm, "Be calm." The second tree realized it was carrying the King of Kings.

The third tree, long forgotten, was now being carried through the streets by a hated man. He was nailed to the tree where He died on the third day. On that hilltop, the tree realized it was mighty and strong, pointing all to God because it supported the crucified Jesus Christ of Nazareth.

The three trees characterize the tree of the knowledge of good and evil, the tree of Calvary and the tree of life in Revelation.[42] They remind us that God sees us and He has a plan for us individually and corporately. And as we endure the valleys of suffering and dashed hopes, our Father patiently shapes us into works of beauty appropriate for His highest purposes.

The Christmas Tree

*Do everything without complaining and arguing,
so that no one can criticize you. Live clean, innocent lives
as children of God, shining like bright lights
in a world full of crooked and perverse people.*
PHILIPPIANS 2:14-15

To many people, Christmastime is a season of cold, busy, and demanding days. It is a season they would rather forget than embrace. Between parties, spending, and uncomfortable family gatherings the joy is overshadowed by anxiety. Thank God for the Christmas tree! Its decorated beauty can illuminate our path to merry and bright.

The Christmas tree is:

A symbol of consistency and beauty. – When all else fails, our inner beauty can continue to shine. *In everything set them an example by doing what is good.* (Titus 2:7)

Fresh and fragrant throughout the year. – Trees that withstand harsh and refreshing conditions grow stronger. Both challenges and peaceful times are welcome. Likewise, we need both challenging and restful times to remain vibrant and help others. *For we are a fragrance of Christ to God among those who are being saved and among those who are perishing.* (2 Corinthians 2:15)

An evergreen tree. – Ever flourishing. *The righteous flourish like the palm tree and grow like a cedar in Lebanon. They are planted in the house of the LORD; they flourish in the courts of our God. They still bear fruit in old age; they are ever full of sap and green.* (Psalms 92:12-14)

Universally and continually relevant. – *Jesus Christ is the same yesterday, today and forever.* (Hebrews 13:8)

Not limited in applicability to a particular event or date. – *Love always protects, always trusts, always hopes, always perseveres.* (1 Corinthians 13:7) *Be thankful in all circumstances.* (1 Thessalonians 5:18)

Let your adorning be the hidden person of the heart with the imperishable beauty of a gentle and quiet spirit, which in God's sight is very precious. (1 Peter 3:4)

On the Count of Tree

A cord of three strands is not quickly broken.
ECCLESIASTES 3:12C

The number three is a significant number to me. I have **three sons** and **three daughters-in-law.**

My three sons have two children each, giving me **three grandsons** and **three granddaughters.**

I have **three sisters, three brothers,** and **three sisters-in-law.**

I was raised by **three**—my **parents** and maternal **grandmother** who lived with us.

My **marriage** is based on **three**—my **husband, myself,** and **God.**

This is my **third** complete **book** and **each chapter** has **three parts.**

I am an **author, speaker,** and **founder** of Community Blend Inc.

Community Blend Inc. is a faith-based nonprofit with three branches—the ***café***, the ***programs***, and the ***missions***.

I wholly depend on the Trinity—***Father, Son*** and ***Holy Spirit*** to lead me through life.

The number three is also significant in the Bible. The Trinity is three in one. The moment of conception is three in one. The meaning of life and eternal hope is found in three: the death, burial, and resurrection of Jesus Christ. Common to all humans are three significant men: Adam, Noah, and Christ. After the Great Flood, Noah's sons, Shem, Ham, and Japheth populated the earth.

These are the generations of the sons of Noah, Shem, Ham, and Japheth. Sons were born to them after the flood. (Genesis 10:1)

These are the clans of the sons of Noah, according to their genealogies, in their nations, and from these the nations spread abroad on the earth after the flood. (Genesis 10:32)

Every human stems from one of these men making all of us related to Noah and each other. We may look different on the outside, and hail from different nations with different tongues, but on the inside we are all part of one race—human.

Everyone has heard the references, "six degrees of separation" and "it's a small world." Six degrees is the theory that all humans are six or less friends away from knowing each other. A small world is the surprise that you and an acquaintance know the same people or meet at an unlikely, distant event.

In the biological and social sciences, the consensus is clear: race is a social construct, not a biological attribute.[43] Genetically speaking there is a 0.1% difference between us.

"The popular classifications of race are based chiefly on

skin color, with other relevant features including height, eyes, and hair. Though these physical differences may appear, on a superficial level, to be very dramatic, they are determined by only a minute portion of the genome: we as a species have been estimated to share 99.9% of our DNA with each other. The few differences that do exist reflect differences in environments and external factors, not core biology."[44]

And that is because we all came from either Ham, Shem, or Japheth.

My three pronouncements on prejudice and racism: It's wrong, it hurts, and it scars.

When I entered the fifth grade, after a summer outdoors, my skin was very dark. We moved to a wealthy neighborhood where I looked different and had a working mom, unlike the ever present, stay-at-home moms of my classmates. Not only was I continually called a racial slur by a mean boy, a few of the moms also treated me as inferior. This only lasted a short time, until I found my style and voice. And in high school that same racist bully wanted to date me. Ugh.

Three final words: *Love Your Neighbor.* (Matthew 22:39)

Reflections

> *But God chose what is foolish in the world to shame the wise;*
> *God chose what is weak in the world to shame the strong;*
> *God chose what is low and despised in the world,*
> *even things that are not, to bring to nothing things that are,*
> *so that no human being might boast in the presence of God.*
> 1 CORINTHIANS 1:27-29

1. As you reflect on the story of *The Three Trees*, how has your life turned out differently from your dreams?

2. What is the benefit of God's plan instead of our way?

3. How would you describe your Christmas celebration?

4. Does knowing we all come from Shem, Ham or Japheth give you a sense of sameness?

5. How can you demonstrate love for your neighbor?

Chapter 14

The Final Three

For an interesting mathematical problem,
visit The Final Three @
https://rb.gy/5f4d7r

The Crooked Tree

An odd scene unfolds as one walks through the forests of Poland. In the center of a common wooded area, sits five acres of deformed pines. This curiosity, rightly named the Crooked Forest, contains 80 trees with a straight top and a hook at the bottom. Many legends attempting to explain this phenomenon exist, but none give an adequate account. My scientific conclusion: No one knows for certain how the weird curve occurred.

The trees, 75-85 years old were planted somewhere between the 1930s to the early 1940s. The 9-foot bend occurs 4 to 20 inches from the ground, shooting up in a straight line thereafter. Some grow in clusters and others sprinkle the forest here and there. But trace evidence shows row plantings, indicating they exist by design.[45]

By design, planted in rows . . . showing someone intended them to be there for a unique purpose. They look different from a typical tree than we expect, but they are indeed trees. Similarly, people who look different are indeed humans, creatively designed and loved by their Creator for a purpose He intended.

No Trees!

Their majestic canopies protect us from the elements, and warm us with fragrances, blooms, and fruit. Trees enhance our lives creatively and physically. As the lungs of the earth they absorb carbon dioxide and release oxygen. Surprisingly there exist places on earth with few or no trees.

Quatar, a country in southwest Asia, has no trees because of its dry climate. The wealthy, urban culture is filled with tall buildings and an award-winning airline, but no abundance of trees. They are righting this wrong by creating the largest man-made forest in the world.

Greenland, from its name, a place that should be filled with greenery is white. A few trees grow in some parts, but plant life is limited because of the harsh wintery conditions.

The *Faroe Islands* are located in the North Atlantic Ocean near Iceland. Natives can boast of their 400 different plant species, but are at a loss when it comes to trees. Naturally treeless, this island has strong winds, gales, and a cool summer climate.

Top: Quatar. Bottom: Faroe Islands.

Haiti, an island in the Caribbean, has the saddest story of all. In a climate where trees would naturally thrive, Haiti fell victim to mass deforestation. Aerial photography from the 40s and 50s shows the devastation. Trees were cut for charcoal, which provides most of their energy. But this deforestation presents a serious problem because a lack of trees causes flooding, erosion, and landslides. In addition, trees fertilize the soil for agriculture, while housing birds and other life.

"Forests are the lungs of our land, purifying the air and giving fresh strength to our people."
President Franklin Roosevelt, 1937

List of State Trees

Did you ever wonder how state symbols originated? The World's Fair of 1893, held in Chicago, stimulated the movement. A national garland of flowers created for the fair carried a unique bloom representing each state. This inspired the implementation of an official state flower throughout the country. The trend led to the adoption of official birds, state icons, mascots, and behold . . . trees. These proud emblems display the unique culture and diversity within the United States.

Trees were chosen because of their contribution to the local economy, usually through the timber trade or as historical landmarks. All are native to the area they represent and flourish in their state, except Hawaii, whose tree originated in Polynesia.

All state symbols, including trees, are adopted through the efforts of local groups who choose objects significant to the state. Historical, social, or academic groups many times lead these charges, researching and presenting noteworthy items for legislative approval.

They wave in the wind, united in purification and beauty as they proudly represent the USA.

Alabama Southern Long Leaf Pine
Alaska Sitka Spruce
Arizona Palo Verde
Arkansas Pine
California Redwood
Colorado Blue Spruce
Connecticut Charter Oak
DC Scarlet Oak
Delaware American Holly
Florida Sabal Palm
Georgia Live Oak
Hawaii Kukui or Candlenut Tree
Idaho Western White Pine
Illinois White Oak
Indiana Tulip Tree
Iowa Oak
Kansas Cottonwood
Kentucky Tulip Poplar
Louisiana Bald Cypress
Maine White Pine
Maryland White Oak
Massachusetts Elm
Michigan White Pine
Minnesota Red or Norway Pine
Mississippi Magnolia
Missouri Flowering Dogwood
Montana Ponderosa Pine
Nebraska Eastern Cottonwood
Nevada Single-Leaf Pinon
New Hampshire White Birch
New Jersey Red Oak
New Mexico Pinon Pine
New York Sugar Maple
North Carolina Pine

North Dakota American Elm
Ohio The Buckeye
Oklahoma Redbud
Oregon Douglas Fir
Pennsylvania Hemlock
Rhode Island Red Maple
South Carolina Palmetto
South Dakota Black Hills Spruce
Tennessee Tulip Poplar
Texas Pecan
Utah Blue Spruce
Vermont Sugar Maple
Virginia American Dogwood
Washington Western Hemlock
West Virginia Sugar Maple
Wisconsin Sugar Maple
Wyoming Plains Cottonwood

Final Reflections

"But blessed are those who trust in the LORD
and have made the LORD their hope and confidence.
They are like trees planted along a riverbank,
with roots that reach deep into the water.
Such trees are not bothered by the heat
or worried by long months of drought.
Their leaves stay green, and they never stop producing fruit.
JEREMIAH 17:7-8

Endnotes

Chapter 1
1. https://www.youtube.com/watch?v=9bAsFMMqq0Q
2. https://www.youtube.com/watch?v=r8hzjNs83nc
   https://sciencing.com/many-types-oak-trees-there-5347784.html

Chapter 2
For a tour visit The Anne Frank House online: https://rb.gy/4rps1q
3. https://www.annefrank.org/en/museum/inside-museum/
4. https://www.guinnessworldrecords.com/world-records/greatest-tree-girth-ever
5. https://www.youtube.com/watch?v=GL1Yw-bNaMM
6. https://saft.wereldboom.org diseased the horse chestnut tree
7. *National Geographic Society,* article-"July 18, CE: Great fire of Rome," October 19, 2023
8. https://www.annefrank.org/en/

Chapter 3
The Thinker – By Auguste Rodin, a French sculptor. The original sculpture from 1904 is in the Musee Rodin in Paris.
9. https://www.atlasobscura.com/places/newtons-apple-tree-trinity-college
10. https://www.christianitytoday.com/history/issues/issue-30/faith-behind-famous-isaac-newton.html
11. Isaac Newton, The Principia: Mathematical Principles of Natural Philosophy https://www.goodreads.com/author/quotes/135106.Isaac_Newton
12. https://libquotes.com/isaac-newton/quote/lbn4z9r

Chapter 4
13. According to his son Kenton Kilmer https://bit.ly/3tfUXOM
14. Letter from Joyce Kilmer to Father James J. Daly, January 9, 1914, in Holliday, Robert Cortes (ed.) and Kilmer, Joyce. *Poems, Essays and Letters in Two Volumes.* (New York: George H. Doran, 1918 – published posthumously).

15 Daly, James Jeremiah. "Some letters of Joyce Kilmer," in his *A Cheerful Ascetic, and Other Essays*. (Milwaukee, Wisconsin: Bruce, 1931), 76-86.
16 Biography of Alfred Joyce Kilmer https://bit.ly/3cBuvcG
17 https://www.poetryfoundation.org/poets/joyce-kilmer
18 https://www.visitnc.com/listing/ZTRS/joyce-kilmer-memorial-forest
19 "Trees" was first published in the August 1913 issue of *Poetry Magazine*.

Chapter 5
20 http://bitly.ws/bF2J
21 Free e-book https://www.planetebook.com/free-ebooks/tess-of-the-durbervilles.pdf
22 http://www.famouspoetsandpoems.com/poets/thomas_hardy/poems/10752
23 https://allpoetry.com/poem/13558571-The-Levelled-Churchyard-by-Thomas-Hardy
24 https://tree-secrets.com/ash-tree/
How to identify an ash tree video: https://tree-secrets.com/ash-tree/

Chapter 6
25 https://bit.ly/3rULcUU
26 https://www.findagrave.com/memorial/904/betsy-ross
27 https://www.findagrave.com/memorial/904/betsy-ross
28 https://www.barna.com/research/americans-are-most-likely-to-base-truth-on-feelings/

Chapter 7
29 https://weirdnj.com/stories/devils-tree/
30 https://backpackerverse.com/heres-why-locals-call-the-devils-tree-a-portal-to-hell/
31 https://www.worldatlas.com/articles/did-you-know-that-there-are-more-trees-on-earth-than-stars-in-the-milky-way.html
https://unbelievable-facts.com/2017/04/trees-and-stars-milky-way.html
32 worldatlas.com 2022
33 https://www.poetryfoundation.org/poems/157984/the-dark-night-of-the-soul

Chapter 8
34 https://bit.ly/3dlm9pE
35 https://lifestylefifty.com/how-many-shoes-should-i-own/

Chapter 9
36 https://localwiki.org/hsl/Paul_Smith's_College
37 https://www.facebook.com/notes/rand-snyder/the-night-of-the-ax-or-the-death-of-an-icon/10150627129496925/
38 Clark F. Mosher This poem originally appeared in the 1971 edition of the *St. Regia.* http://pscpubs.paulsmiths.edu/lccn/sn89038522/1986-01-01/ed-1/seq-7.pdf
39 Statement, Bouton to state police, notarized-public document, New York state, Essex County, North Elba, March 8, 1972; found in Woods' history of the college, p. 184

Chapter 10
40 https://t.ly/XIDj8, Paradox interactive

Chapter 11
41 New England Historical Society, https://bitly.ws/38rYU, WHY CONNECTICUT SENT HENRY OBOOKIAH BACK TO HAWAII, 175 YEARS AFTER HE DIED, article updated 2023.
An Interesting Read: The Long Journey Home, by Nick Bellantoni, The Repatriations of Henry Opukaha'ia and Albert Afraid of Hawk, https://bitly.ws/38s2L

Chapter 13
42 The origin of The Tale of Three Trees is unknown.
43 https://sitn.hms.harvard.edu/flash/2017/science-genetics-reshaping-race-debate-21st-century/
44 This work by SITNBoston is licensed under a Creative Commons Attribution-NonCommercial-ShareAlike 4.0 International License.

Chapter 14
45 https://duckduckgo.com/?q=The%20crooked%20forest&ko=-1&ia=web&iax=about/ https://www.historicmysteries.com/crooked-forest-poland/ Epoch Times Polska. June 01, 2018. Accessed January 15, 2019.

All scripture is taken from the ESV, NIV and NLT (unless otherwise noted) online from www.Biblehub.com and www.biblestudytools.com.

Graphics credits including coloring pages:

Online sources free and printable: Getty Images, Pixabay, https://rb.gy/toiant, https://rb.gy/p7xnb.

Good Free Photos – All public domain pictures of plants and trees.

British Library – Over a million images, taken mostly from illustrations in 17th, 18th and 19th century books, released into the public domain.

Pixnio – A large collection of high-resolution public domain images. Free for personal and commercial use, no attribution required.

Wikimedia Commons hosts over 6.2 million public domain images, the largest free "images-only" repository.

Devostock.com – Over 160,000 free professional images for commercial use.

Flickr Public Domain Search – About 6 million Public Domain images ("No known copyright restrictions" and "U.S. Gov't Works"). Includes British Library.

Free-Images.com – More than 12 Million Public Domain/CC0 stock images, clip-art, historical photos and more. Commercial use OK. No attribution required. No login required.

Branches of Thanksgiving

To my dear sister Maureen Brackshaw, for her tireless hours spent editing my book. You are a treasure to behold and the most disciplined person I know. Thank you for your love, tender guidance, and support. I love our friendship and sisterhood.

To my devoted husband Craig, who patiently reads my chapters and answers my questions.

To Sharon Denton for her beautiful artwork on the dedication page, The Family Tree. Your mentorship over many years has called me to a greater understanding of God, myself, and the Word.

To the *Behold a Tree* prayer team: Bobbie Rodriquez, Sharon Denton, Val Sarkady, Carol Skibenes. You are the foundation and support in developing these ideas. Thank you! Your faithfulness and input over many years is a gift.

To my beta readers: Val Sarkady, Diane Obrien, Craig Utt, and reviewers: Ralph Fiore, Ron Collins, Daryl Detrick, Kathy Halpin, Deb Gatz, Toni Samuels, thank you for taking the time to read my chapters. Your words mean so much.

To Ron Collins for sharing your college story with me. The sadness of your loss, evident after so many years, makes this story as special as you.

To my siblings Maureen, Jerome, Marigold, Bobbie, and Dale who pray for me daily, share Bible verses, and who are involved in my decision making. And to my siblings-in-law, who share love and life with my siblings and my husband, Margaret, Tony, Tom - Loren, Julie, Jeff. We are a special family.

To the contributors of *Tree of Life Stories*: Barbara Sako, Joyce Livelli, Jennifer Prystash, Diane O'Brien, Faith Craft, Deb Gatz, Beth Brubaker. Thank you for taking the time to share your stories.

Community Blend Incorporated

Community Blend is a faith-based mission to assist people in need and provide avenues for the community to learn, serve, and belong. Not limited to the local area, Community Blend has helped families in eight other states . . . so far. The nonprofit has three main branches—the café, the programs, and the mission.

The Café serves specialty coffee, bakery goods, and novelty items at no cost. People can work remotely, gather with friends, or sit quietly and read. It also provides a space for other community nonprofits and groups to hold their meetings.

The Programs include academic, social, spiritual, accredited, physical, and need-based offerings. Most are free, but for those that have a charge, excluding the accredited, anyone can participate for free if they cannot afford the cost.

The Mission assists people in crisis helping them to restore their situation. A pay-it-forward program allows recipients to volunteer at the café.

A portion of the proceeds for this book will go to the work Community Blend is doing locally and nationally. We thrive on your prayers and financial support. Check us out at Communityblend.org.

Visit the author's page "Passion, Purpose, Promise" @ Jewellutt.com.

About the Author

JEWELL is dedicated to serving her community and connecting people to God and each other. As an author, speaker, and the director of a nonprofit mission, she pursues her calling to encourage people and assist those in need. Knowing she is an imperfect person in an imperfect world makes her ever grateful to God for His direction and grace

The mountainous area where she lives with her husband Craig, provides a range of creative opportunities to write about the magnificence of nature and how it uplifts our spirits. She is surrounded by excellence through her husband, sons, daughters-in-law, siblings, and in-laws. The wisdom they pour into her life through their example is the root of her ministry.

More by Jewell Utt

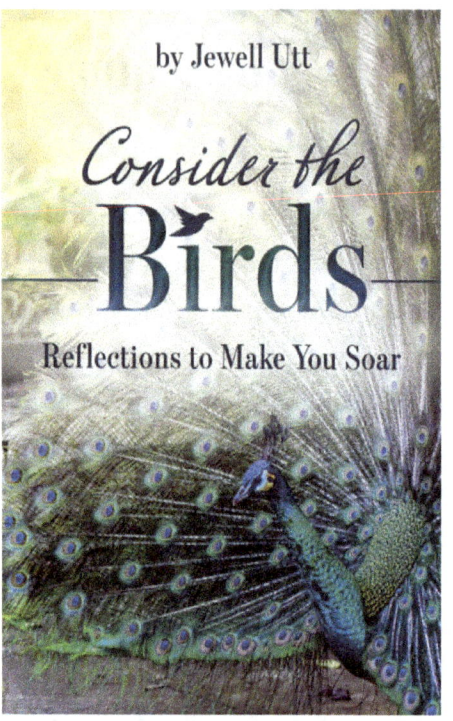

The author introduces a unique parallel between man and birds. Her reflections will stimulate your devotional time, lead you into intimacy with God, and inspire you to soar to new heights. Each chapter presents: surprising and unique bird behavior; similar characteristics found in humans; Biblical and personal stories showcasing shared behavior; accounts to inspire personal reflection; and questions to motivate change and help you soar. *(130pp. color illus. Masthof Press, 2019.) $12*

www.ingramcontent.com/pod-product-compliance
Lightning Source LLC
Chambersburg PA
CBHW070104080526
44586CB00013B/1175